The Essential Buyer's Guide

CHEVROLET
CORVETTE C6

2005 to 2013

Your marque expert:
David Smitheram

VELOCE
FINE AUTOMOTIVE BOOKS

The Essential Buyer's Guide Series

Alfa Romeo Alfasud (Metcalfe)
Alfa Romeo Alfetta: all saloon/sedan models 1972 to 1984 & coupé models 1974 to 1987 (Metcalfe)
Alfa Romeo Giulia GT Coupé (Booker)
Alfa Romeo Giulia Spider (Booker)
Audi TT (Davies)
Audi TT Mk2 2006 to 2014 (Durnan)
Austin-Healey Big Healeys (Trummel)
BMW E30 3 Series 1981 to 1994 (Hosier)
BMW X5 (Saunders)
BMW Z3 Roadster (Fishwick)
BMW Z4: E85 Roadster and E86 Coupé including M and Alpina 2003 to 2009 (Smitheram)
Citroën 2CV (Paxton)
Citroën DS & ID (Heilig)
Cobra Replicas (Ayre)
Corvette C2 Sting Ray 1963-1967 (Falconer)
Datsun 240Z 1969 to 1973 (Newlyn)
DeLorean DMC-12 1981 to 1983 (Williams)
FIAT 124 Spider & Pininfarina Azzura Spider, (AS-DS) 1966 to 1985 (Robertson)
Fiat 500 & 600 (Bobbitt)
Ford Capri (Paxton)
Ford Escort Mk1 & Mk2 (Williamson)
Ford Focus Mk1 RS & ST170, 1st Generation (Williamson)
Ford Model A – All Models 1927 to 1931 (Buckley)
Ford Model T – All models 1909 to 1927 (Barker)
Ford Mustang – First Generation 1964 to 1973 (Cook)
Ford Mustang – 3rd generation: 1979-1993; inc Mercury Capri: 1979-1986 (Smith)
Ford Mustang – Fifth Generation (2005-2014) (Cook)
Ford RS Cosworth Sierra & Escort (Williamson)
Hillman Imp (Morgan)
Hinckley Triumph triples & fours 750, 900, 955, 1000, 1050, 1200 – 1991-2009 (Henshaw)
Jaguar E-Type 3.8 & 4.2 litre (Crespin)
Jaguar E-type V12 5.3 litre (Crespin)
Jaguar Mark 1 & 2 (All models including Daimler 2.5-litre V8) 1955 to 1969 (Thorley)
Jaguar New XK 2005-2014 (Thorley)
Jaguar S-Type – 1999 to 2007 (Thorley)
Jaguar X-Type – 2001 to 2009 (Thorley)
Jaguar XJ-S (Crespin)
Jaguar XJ6, XJ8 & XJR (Thorley)
Jaguar XK 120, 140 & 150 (Thorley)
Jaguar XK8 & XKR (1996-2005) (Thorley)
Jaguar/Daimler XJ 1994-2003 (Crespin)
Jaguar/Daimler XJ40 (Crespin)
Jaguar/Daimler XJ6, XJ12 & Sovereign (Crespin)
Lancia Delta HF 4WD & Integrale (Baker)
Land Rover Discovery Series 1 (1989-1998) (Taylor)
Land Rover Discovery Series 2 (1998-2004) (Taylor)
Land Rover Series I, II & IIA (Thurman)
Land Rover Series III (Thurman)
Lotus Elan, S1 to Sprint and Plus 2 to Plus 2S 130/5 1962 to 1974 (Vale)
Lotus Europa, S1, S2, Twin-cam & Special 1966 to 1975 (Vale)
Lotus Seven replicas & Caterham 7: 1973-2013 (Hawkins)
Mazda MX-5 Miata (Mk1 1989-97 & Mk2 98-2001) (Crook)
Mazda MX-5 Miata (Mk3, 3.5 & 3.75 models, 2005-2015) (Wild)
Mazda RX-8 (Parish)
Mercedes-Benz 190: all 190 models (W201 series) 1982 to 1993 (Parish)
Mercedes-Benz 280-560SL & SLC (Bass)
Mercedes-Benz G-Wagen (Greene)
Mercedes-Benz Pagoda 230SL, 250SL & 280SL roadsters & coupés (Bass)
Mercedes-Benz S-Class W126 Series (Zoporowski)
Mercedes-Benz S-Class Second Generation W116 Series (Parish)
Mercedes-Benz SL R129-series 1989 to 2001 (Parish)
Mercedes-Benz SLK (Bass)
Mercedes-Benz W123 (Parish)
Mercedes-Benz W124 – All models 1984-1997 (Zoporowski)
MG Midget & A-H Sprite (Horler)
MG TD, TF & TF1500 (Jones)
MGA 1955-1962 (Crosier)
MGB & MGB GT (Williams)
MGF & MG TF (Hawkins)
Mini (Paxton)
Morgan 4/4 (Benfield)
Morgan Plus 4 (Benfield)
Morgan Plus 8 (Benfield)
Morris Minor & 1000 (Newell)
New Mini (Collins)
Peugeot 205 GTI (Blackburn)
Porsche 356 (Johnson)
Porsche 911 (964) (Streather)
Porsche 911 (991) (Streather)
Porsche 911 (993) (Streather)
Porsche 911 (996) (Streather)
Porsche 911 (997) – Model years 2004 to 2009 (Streather)
Porsche 911 (997) – Second generation models 2009 to 2012 (Streather)
Porsche 911 Carrera 3.2 (Streather)
Porsche 911SC (Streather)
Porsche 924 – All models 1976 to 1988 (Hodgkins)
Porsche 928 (Hemmings)
Porsche 930 Turbo & 911 (930) Turbo (Streather)
Porsche 944 (Higgins)
Porsche 981 Boxster & Cayman (Streather)
Porsche 986 Boxster (Streather)
Porsche 987 Boxster and Cayman 1st generation (2005-2009) (Streather)
Porsche 987 Boxster and Cayman 2nd generation (2009-2012) (Streather)
Range Rover – First Generation models 1970 to 1996 (Taylor)
Range Rover – Second Generation 1994-2001 (Taylor)
Range Rover – Third Generation L322 (2002-2012) (Taylor)
Reliant Scimitar GTE (Payne)
Rolls-Royce Silver Shadow & Bentley T-Series (Bobbitt)
Rover 2000, 2200 & 3500 (Marrocco)
Subaru Impreza (Hobbs)
Sunbeam Alpine (Barker)
Triumph Herald & Vitesse (Ayre)
Triumph Spitfire and GT6 (Ayre)
Triumph Stag (Mort)
Triumph TR2 & TR3 – All models (including 3A & 3B) 1953 to 1962 (Conners)
Triumph TR4/4A & TR5/250 – All models 1961 to 1968 (Child & Battyll)
Triumph TR6 (Williams)
Triumph TR7 & TR8 (Williams)
TVR Chimaera and Griffith (Kitchen)
TVR S-series (Kitchen)
Volkswagen Bus (Copping)
Volkswagen Transporter T4 (1990-2003) (Copping/Cservenka)
VW Golf GTI (Copping)
VW Beetle (Copping)
Volvo 700/900 Series (Beavis)
Volvo P1800/1800S, E & ES 1961 to 1973 (Murray)

www.veloce.co.uk

First published in 2025 by Veloce, an imprint of David and Charles Limited.
Tel +44 (0)1305 260068 / e-mail info@veloce.co.uk / web www.veloce.co.uk.

ISBN: 9781787119192
 Readers with ideas for automotive books, or books on other transport or related hobby subjects, are invited to write to the editorial director of Veloce at the above email address. British Library Cataloguing in Publication Data – A catalogue record for this book is available from the British Library.
Design and production by Veloce. Printed and bound in the UK by Short Run Press Ltd.

Introduction
– the purpose of this book

The Chevrolet Corvette C6, and its now legendary LS V8 engine, is the perfect antidote to today's uninspiring and complicated cars. This Essential Buyer's Guide combines expert, first-hand experience with clear color photos to ensure you avoid buying a lemon, and instead get to enjoy one of the most versatile two-seat sports cars in the world.

This book will guide you through the choosing and buying process, helping you understand and compare the various models, before selecting the best C6 for your budget, pointing out common and potential problem areas along the way.

Coupe or Convertible?

My C6 has travelled across the States, down to the Sahara Desert in Africa, around Europe, and in the Arctic, along the most northerly highway in the world.

It has won championships on the track, and has delivered exceptional reliability and cost-effectiveness. I have found the C6 an easy sports car to work on, with good parts availability, plenty of tuning potential, support from specialists, and a keen enthusiast following.

Road trip to the Sahara Desert.

In this era of social media and the internet, there is a wealth of information available, but it can take hours and days to establish what are the genuine, common issues to look for. The purpose of this book is to cut through the often-repeated myths and one-off breakages and give you a real-world, condensed source of what to look for in a C6.

Background
On its launch in 1997, the C5 set a new benchmark for Corvette design and engineering, with the now legendary 5.7-liter LS1 'small block' engine. The C5's hydroformed steel chassis was considerably more rigid and lighter than that of the C4, allowing for enhanced suspension tuning. Design cues, like pop-up headlights and the interior were due a refresh, the racing programme would benefit from an updated model, too.

When the C6 was launched in 2004, for the 2005 model year (MY), some commentators suggested that the C6 could actually have been called a C5.5, such was the close evolution of chassis design and parts sharing. It appears Corvette kept the best bits of the C5 and improved on them, keeping the weight and cost down, too. The design was all-new, with shorter overhangs (by 5.1in) and more European styling cues. The return of circular rear lights was welcomed, as was the contemporary interior design.

With each new C6 model year came changes and improvements, some small, others significant, with greater choice of body type, equipment, special editions and increased engine capacity and power. The Z06's LS7 set a power record for GM in 2006, at 505hp. This was later beaten by the ZR1, its supercharged LS9 producing 638hp and a record for the fastest production car lap around the Nürburgring, with a 7:26.4, bettered again in 2012. The C6R racing programme enjoyed great success worldwide, with championship and Le Mans victories.

The global financial crisis, starting in 2008, saw production figures cruelly slump, despite the introduction of the ZR1, Grand Sport and 427 models. The Corvette C7 took over for the 2014 MY and, whilst it certainly raised the bar, particularly in interior quality, some say that the C6 is the peak blend of reliability, simplicity, power and comfort.

All Corvette C6s were built at the Bowling Green, Kentucky plant. The rare and desirable Callaway Corvettes were further assembled at its Connecticut, California or German facilities.

Corvette C5. (Courtesy Mark Eaton)

Round lights return

Callaway Convertible. (Courtesy Nigel Dobbie)

Road tests

Road tests generally loved the C6, in all variants.

Car and Driver, on the 2005 Z51: "It's the perfect everything sports car: fast enough to keep you interested during a day of lapping and refined and comfortable enough to make the slog home, or the daily commute, a relaxing experience. Take any sports car within 20 grand of the Corvette's sticker, and the Vette will flat smoke it."

In 2020, *Road and Track* looked back at the C6 range: "With a near 50-50 weight distribution and a curb weight just under 3250 pounds, it's a blast to drive, right out of the box."

Contents

The Essential Buyer's Guide™ currency
At the time of publication a BG unit of currency "●" equals approximately US$ 1.00/£0.80/Euro 0.90. Please adjust to suit current exchange rates.

1 Is it the right car for you?

– marriage guidance

The enduring appeal of a Corvette C6 stems from its versatility. Whatever you could reasonably want a sports car for, it can do it well. Road tripping for two with a trunk full of luggage, tearing up the track or heading to the store, the C6 can do it all in style and with character. The V8 engine dominates the experience, of course: the smoothness, power and the engine note represent the epitome of a large American sports car.

America's sportscar.

Every Corvette C6 has two comfortable leather seats, a simple, gasoline powered pushrod V8 engine, rear-wheel drive with limited slip differential, head turning looks and thrilling handling.

Transmission, power and body

The C6 came with a choice of four V8 engines, from 400hp to 638hp, manual or

C6 is small by comparison to many modern cars

automatic transmissions, and five different body styles, with narrow- or wide-body Convertibles, narrow- or wide-body targa-roof Coupe, and wide-body fixed-roof Coupe.

Size

Interior space is accommodating to a wide variety of driver heights and weights. The C6 is low to get into, but doors open widely. Visibility is good, storage (especially in the Coupe) is ample.

Rivals

Given the versatility, value for money and performance range of the C6, it's actually quite difficult to make a direct comparison with other cars. Rivals are usually more expensive, both to buy and run, or their handling is blunted by a high curb weight.

Camaro 5th generation.

Mustang S550 may be newer, but better?

Chevrolet's fifth generation Camaro offered the same engines and added rear seats, but at a higher weight and with less visibility out of the cabin. Greater production numbers reduced their exclusivity, with the Ford Mustang and Dodge Challenger and Charger also suffering from high mass. All lack the C6's sleek sports car physique.

The Dodge Viper and Lotus Elise are not as friendly to use on a daily basis. Exotics from Italy prove far more costly to run, and are typically not as robust, or reliable.

AMG offers a V8 soundtrack, but in automatic only.

The Porsche 911, Cayman or Boxster have fantastic brakes and handling, but their engines offer less power and have well-known issues pre-2009, and they have overly long gearing. Parts and servicing are more expensive.

BMW Z4Ms lack a V8 option and are manual only. BMW M3s are a popular choice, although the E46 semi-automatic is jerky. The M3 E90/E92 is heavier than a C6, its V8 is a high-revving, smaller capacity engine, and lacks torque relative to the Corvette LS engines. M-engine rod bearings of this era can be prone to wear.

Japan's Honda S2000 and Mazda Miata deliver affordable running costs and top-down thrills, but their four-cylinder engines lack grunt and aural variety. Rust can be a problem, too.

The two-seat Cadillac XLR shared some parts with the C6, including its hydroformed chassis, and was even built at the same Bowling Green factory, but was automatic only, and came with the smaller capacity Northstar V8 engine.

Perhaps the C6's greatest rivals are other models of Corvette. The C5 is older and typically cheaper, whilst the slightly more complex C7, being newer, is still likely to depreciate further.

Racing C6 and C7R.

2 Cost considerations

– affordable, or a money pit?

This is an area in which the C6 excels. Resale values are strong, cars are reliable, and common replacement parts are readily available and well-priced.

The pushrod LS engine is robust and simple, highly tuneable, over-engineered, and capable of considerable power increases, even on stock components. In fact, there's a previous generation C5 currently in the National Corvette Museum (NCM) with 773,338 miles on the original LS1 engine!

LS engines are very reliable.

Servicing

Services alternate between Maintenance 1 and Maintenance 2 lists. The Driver Information Center (DIC) counts down oil health as a percentage, depending on how the car is used. The % oil life could be as short as 3000 miles to longer than 15,000 miles. All C6s left the factory with 5W30 fully synthetic oil.

If you are confident with a spanner, the oil drain plug, oil filter, cabin filter and air filter are all accessible with the car raised by just a small amount.

Parts

Chevrolet dealers are competitively priced for many parts, with some having online or eBay stores. Owners overseas may not have local dealer support in their country, but the companies listed in chapter 16 offer rapid worldwide shipping.

Chevrolet dealers can be well-priced for parts.

Tires

All Corvette C6s have wide, large diameter tires (originally runflats), with no spare wheel. For reasons of cost, availability and comfort, in most cases the runflats have been replaced with conventional tires. As you start to enjoy the power at your disposal, it's not uncommon to replace rear tires at twice the rate of the front pair!

Gas mileage

Thanks to an aerodynamic shape and light weight, Corvette C6 can be surprisingly fuel efficient in the real world. EPA figures vary between 15mpg (US) city, 19 combined and 26 highway, with Z06 wide-body or automatics getting slightly less than a manual, narrow-body.

All C6s must use top tier gas to avoid potentially damaging pre-detonation and a loss of performance.

Example parts GM/AC Delco unless mentioned, US online sources.

Part	Price
Front Z51 rotor (each)	x70
Front Z51 pads (axle set)	x50
Front Z06 FE4 damper	x84
Front Z06 Magnetic Ride Control damper	x425
Oil filter	x5
Air filter elements (pair)	x15
Cabin filter	x14
Rear Z06 wheel bearing, hub and studs	x162
Rear tire Coupe/Convertible 285/35/19 Yokohama	x256
Rear tire Z06 325/30/19 Yokohama	x324

3 Living with a C6 Corvette

– will you get along together?

The C6 is an easy car to live with. It has few vices, as long as you buy the right one. Putting budget aside, a Z06 or ZR1 might not be the most comfortable choice for a daily driver, whilst a 2005 four-speed auto Convertible isn't the fastest at the track.

A modified Z06 is rapid on the track.

Will it fit?

Corvette C6s are low, relatively wide sports cars. Their ride height can be easily lowered or raised on the stock monoleaf springs, but may still scrape on steep approaches or curbs (crossing dips or rises at an angle can help). Wide-bodied cars are 3.3in wider than standard/narrow-body cars. The extra width comes from wider, offset wheels with flared body arches. The chassis and suspension are the same dimensions. You can quickly identify a wide-bodied car by the center vent beside the front badge and the brake ducts in front of the rear wheels.

Drivers of most sizes and weights can fit. (Courtesy Felix Page)

Driver/passenger fit and comfort

All models feature comfortable electric, leather or leather/microsuede seats, all with the same frame and base foam. Higher trim levels/options can gain heater elements, an electric passenger seat, steering column reach/tilt, memory settings, two-tone and microsuede inserts and stitched logos, with the optional 'sports' seats gaining powered side bolsters and multi-piece back foam.

They all have disappointing lateral support that will leave you clinging to the wheel as you power through turns. This was only partially improved with the sports seat option, and the later (2012-on) square-shouldered design. Both seat backs hinge forward, for rear access behind.

Late model seat.

All C6s left the factory with composite, transverse monoleaf springs. These are not 'cart springs', but highly effective, long-lasting, lightweight springs. Non-Z51 Coupe and Convertible are the softest ride, but enthusiastic driving will soon reveal body roll and pitch. Springs, sway bars and dampers can be swapped between models. Cars with Z51 performance pack, or the Grand Sport are firmer, but still comfortable on the road.

Damping was controlled by conventional, non-adjustable, gas-filled shocks or selective Magnetic Ride Control. The latter allows an instant change from sport to tour mode via a dial on the center console. A common upgrade is to remove the monoleaf springs and separate shocks, and replace them with a coilover setup.

Magnetic Ride Control.

Equipment

Even the base trim level cars come well equipped. A head-up display (HUD), which projects speed and other information onto the windshield, is standard on all but the base trim levels.

All years came with a CD player that will play MP3 discs (needs a dealer reflash to do so on 05 cars), an optional 3.5mm aux was added in 08, USB from 2011.

Bluetooth was an option from 2009, but is for handsfree calling only, not music streaming.

Head-up display.

Noise

A big part of the appeal of the C6 is that V8 engine note. The stock mufflers are drone-free, but far too quiet for many, something that Corvette improved from 2008 with the 2.5in NPP option, which has butterfly valves in the exhaust. This achieved a best-of-both-worlds, quiet and noisier function, with a small power boost of 6hp, too. A similar, but larger 3in Bi-mode exhaust was standard on the Z06 and ZR1. You can pull a 10-amp fuse to remain in louder mode. The dual-mode mufflers can be retrofitted to earlier cars with a 'mild to wild' box.

Fortunately, if you want more aural drama, aftermarket headers and mufflers are a popular upgrade.

Perfect condition Grand Sport Coupe, with trunk open.

Storage

The trunk in the C6 Coupe is large at 22 cubic feet, compared to other sports cars. Wet-sump engine C6 Corvettes have two storage compartments in the rear corners, below the height of the trunk floor (useful for a quart of oil, basic tools, cleaning equipment, etc). Dry-sump engine C6 Corvettes, like the ZR1, Z06, and six-speed manual Grand Sport Coupes, have one storage compartment (the battery is stored in the other).

Coupe trunk with cargo shade.

Convertible trunk.

The glovebox is of average size. There are two drinks holders in the center console (hidden by a tambour door), these will hold a pair of standard-size drinks cans. A shallow storage area beneath the hinged armrest can get hot, so don't store your phone or candy here! There are two 12v sockets.

Coupes can swallow the most luggage, enough for two for a multi-week vacation, or multiple sets of golf clubs. When the removable targa roof (where applicable) is stowed in the trunk, available access and space is greatly reduced. The Coupe trunk is open to the cabin, with a low lip stopping loose items rolling forwards; this can be useful for a passenger to reach back for a bag whilst moving. Partitions and dividers are available as an accessory.

The Convertible's trunk may be half the volume of the Coupe at 11 cubic feet (varies slightly when the hood is lowered or raised), but it can still swallow two sets of golf clubs, which is impressive. The trunk is sealed off from the cabin. Additional small storage bins are located behind the Convertible seats.

Left-hand/right-hand drive C6

All Chevrolet Corvette C6s left the factory as left-hand drive. A handful of right-hand drive conversions exist, all performed by independent companies, mostly in Australia. These will need to be carefully considered and checked, but could command a significant premium.

4 Relative values
– which model for you?

When sifting through adverts it's important to understand the difference between the various C6 models, packages, trim levels, individual options and special editions. The myriad combinations changed on an annual basis, and listing them is beyond the scope of this Essential Buyer's Guide. To avoid any doubt, the build sticker, located in the glovebox lid, has a list of all the factory codes.

Narrow/standard-body Coupe, also known as 'base'.

The most numerous model sold was the Coupe, with a removable targa roof on a steel chassis. These are sometimes known as the 'base' model, although that was never a term used by Chevrolet, and won't be used much in this book. Next most common is the narrow, fabric roof Convertible. Both are available in 6- and 6.2-liter flavors, with manual or automatic transmissions, with or without the Z51 performance package. For ease of differentiation, we'll call these 'base' models narrow width or standard width.

Grand Sport Convertible.

The high-performance Z06 has the wide-body on alloy chassis, with magnesium subframes, a 7-liter dry-sumped engine, in manual only. Although the roof is fixed in place, it can be unbolted, but this is not something Chevrolet envisaged.

The Grand Sport came later, with the wide-body looks, brakes and tires of the Z06, but on a steel chassis, 6.2-liter engine (dry-sumped on manual cars), and the choice of removable targa roof or fabric Convertible and manual or automatic transmissions.

The ZR1 'King Of The Hill' is the wide-bodied monster, with dry-sumped 6.2-liter supercharged powerplant through a manual gearbox, with fixed roof, and on an alloy chassis.

The low-numbers 427 came late in the life of the C6. Wide-bodied, steel-framed, fabric-roof Convertible, with the Z06 7-liter engine and manual transmission only.

Terminology

Model examples are:

Coupe, Convertible, Grand Sport, Z06, and so on.

Packages include (to name just a few):

Z51 pack for the Coupe/Convertible, that includes different gearbox ratios, transmission cooling, stiffer springs, dampers and sway bars, plus larger rotors.
Z07 pack for the Z06 contains most of the ZR1 upgrades, for example, carbon-ceramic brakes, exhaust, enhanced cooling and suspension, bigger wheels and, in some years, more carbonfiber panels but without the supercharged engine.
Grand Sport Heritage pack adds fender stripes and two-tone leather.

Trim levels

These typically describe the interior specification and equipment levels, not the way the car performs.

2005 had three trim levels, 1SX (equivalent to 1LT), 1SB (2LT) and 2SB (3LZ). Note that this range of trim level lettering continued in the Canadian market, beyond 2005.
2006-on Coupe, Convertible and Grand Sport start at 1LT, through to the best equipped 4LT.
Z06 start at 1LZ, through to the best equipped 3LZ.
ZR1 had two trim levels, 1ZR and 3ZR.
427 had three trim levels, 1SA, 1SB, 1SC.

As an example of trim levels on USA market, narrow-bodied Coupe and Convertible:

1LT – Coupe includes: six-speed manual, and, from 2006, a six-speed auto. Stereo CD XM, MP3 jack starting in 2008, OnStar (no longer works), leather seats, six-way power driver seat, active handling traction control, dual zone A/C, keyless access/start, foglamps, manual tilt (but not reach) steering wheel, cruise control, tire pressure monitor (TPMS), body color removable top, and power hatch release with power pull down.

1LT 2007 Coupe, note lack of HUD buttons to left of steering wheel.

Leather wrapped dash, a touch of luxury but check for lifting.

1LT Convertible includes power trunk release and manual top; side air bags, sport seats, power passenger seat, cargo net.
2LT Coupe includes all of the 1LT pack, plus seat-mounted side impact air bags, sport seats, six-way power passenger seat, cargo net and cargo shade.
3LT Coupe and Convertible all of 1LT and 2LT options, plus HUD, power telescopic steering column, memory package, heated seats, auto-dimming inside and outside mirrors, compass in rear-view mirror, USB 6CD radio with BOSE seven speaker system, steering wheel audio controls, universal home remote transmitter, power top for Convertibles.

The 4LT added custom leather wrapped interior.

In 2012, extras were added to the 2LT options including Nav Radio, BOSE, Bluetooth, USB, and HUD. 4LT, 3LZ, 3ZR and Centennial Editions could come equipped with the custom leather package, with microsuede inserts on the seats, steering wheel, center console cover/armrest with more padding, shift knob and shift boot, in addition to leather wrapped dash, upper door trim panels and model-specific headrest embroidery.

Specification of C6s officially sold overseas may differ. For example, European cars were typically Z51-packaged 3LT models with headlight washers, rear fog lights, side indicators and different rear lights.

European Z06 with headlight washers.

Optional caliper covers over the smaller JL9 rotors.

Individual and dealer options could be chosen from the sales brochure and varied through the years. These included caliper color, dual mode performance exhaust, embroidered head rests, wheels, Magnetic Ride Control, translucent top, and more.

Special edition cars, like the Z06 Carbon and Ron Fellows Pace car replicas, ZHZ Hertz, 60th and Centennial anniversary cars, have a specific equipment level from the factory that could be added to.

2009 GT1 Edition. (Courtesy Nigel Dobbie)

Body style?

This is an alternative, simple way of seeing the range of body styles available:

Narrow-body Coupe, with removable targa roof panel, sometimes described as the 'base'.
Wide-body Coupe, with removable targa roof panel, Grand Sport.
Wide-body Coupe, fixed roof, alloy chassis, Z06 and ZR1.
Narrow-body Convertible, with fabric top.
Wide-body Convertible, with fabric top, Grand Sport, 427.

Transmission: automatic or manual?

All models were available with a six-speed manual transmission. Automatic transmissions were a popular option on the narrow-body Coupe, Convertible and Grand Sport, but never available on the highest performance models (the Z06, 427 and ZR1), which were manual only.

All automatics fitted were of a 'Hydra-Matic' torque-converting type, providing a smooth, reliable, if not particularly fast shift (by today's standards). The first year, 2005, auto was a four-speed. All other years were a six-speed, with manual change added to steering wheel buttons.

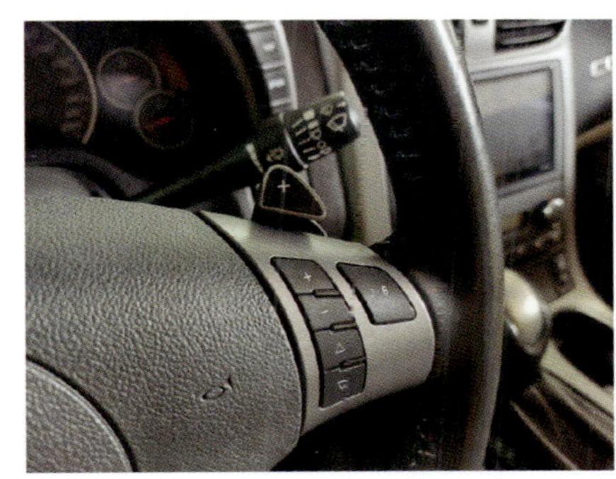

Steering wheel paddle shift on 2006+ automatics.

The gearbox, along with the standard-fit limited-slip differential, is mounted in the rear of the vehicle, for better packaging and weight distribution. Whilst they are bolted together, their fluids are separate, so they're not a true transaxle.

Which engine?

The fourth generation LS engines are all-alloy, V8, gasoline, pushrod, with

Rear mounted transmission.

two valves per cylinder. Thankfully none were ever fitted with the occasionally problematic cylinder deactivation, as fitted to the later C7.
LS2, 6-liter, 400hp, 2005 to 2007, narrow-body Coupe and Convertible.
LS3, 6.2-liter, 430hp, 2008 to 2013, narrow-body Coupe, Convertible and Grand Sport.
LS7, 7-liter, 505hp, from 2006 to 2013, Z06 and 427 Convertible.
LS9, 6.2-liter supercharged, 638hp, 2009 to 2013, ZR1.

Wet-sumped LS2 and LS3 engines were built in St Catharines, Ontario. Dry-sumped, LS3 (Grand Sport manual), LS7 and LS9 engines were hand-assembled in Wixom, Michigan, with signed name plates near the intake manifold.

5 Before you view

– be well informed

Is there a year, or engine to avoid?

In a word, no. First year, 2005, cars are unfairly singled out by some. Yes, the four-speed automatic is not as sporting as the later six-speed, the differentials are not as robust under hard use, and the '05 does have some unique quirks, parts and a different steering wheel, but is still a good car and shouldn't be overlooked if the price is right.

The LS2 and LS3 are every bit as reliable as each other, stock or modified, but the LS3 heads and intake flow a greater volume of air, if greater power is the aim.

Corvette chief engineer Tadge Juechter said "Corvette is the poster child for continuous improvement. Making our car look, feel and perform better is what we do every day."

2005 only steering wheel, here wrapped in suede.

Be careful where you meet the seller, ideally somewhere well lit.

Team Banana
Motorsports
Louis Latour
54
P1
KANSAS
CB54 VET
TAITTINGER
Reims
RACING LEGENDS

Highly modified C6.

2007 Indy Pace Car replica is a true collectable.

Condition (body/chassis/interior/mechanicals)?

Ask for an honest appraisal of the car's condition. What is less than perfect (every used car has imperfections)? Ask specifically about some of the items described in chapter 7. Realistic expectations should be set based on the mileage and asking price.

All original specification or modified?

An unmodified car can be of the same or higher value than a customized version, but this really depends on what has been modified and what your preferences are.

What year?

For the benefit of perspective owners outside of the USA, the model year isn't necessarily the actual year of production. A Corvette model year typically runs from June/July, so when a C6 is advertised as a 2008, it could have actually left the production line from mid-2007 onwards, but in 2008 specification. Throughout this guide, any year quoted is the model year.

Limited numbers/collectors' cars

Whilst there are low numbers, collectors' cars, you will need to decide if the '1 of 462 made in this color and upholstery in 2006' is worth any kind of premium to you. It may not be 'rare', just a result of the way it was ordered and built, with the thousands of different permutations.

Matching data/legal ownership/money

Does the seller hold the title in their name? Is there any finance outstanding? Clean title? Accident or theft history? Annual test of roadworthiness? Smog/emissions certificate? A current road fund licence/licence plate tag? Ask how the seller might want to be paid, if a deal were to be struck?

Professional vehicle check/pre-purchase inspection

For peace of mind, particularly if you are not confident, or unable to give the car a thorough check over, you may consider an independent inspection. A Corvette owners club/group, AAA or Corvette specialist may be able to help. The internet will reveal others, who specifically perform this sort of mobile, pre-purchase inspection.

6 Inspection equipment

– these items will really help

Before you rush out of the door, gather together a few items that will help as you work your way around the car.

This book
Reading glasses (if you need them for close work)
Flashlight
Overalls, or clothes you won't mind if they get a little dirt on
Something comfortable to kneel or lay on
Mirror on a 'stick' and/or borescope
Magnet
A clean paper towel, or cloth
Camera phone (handheld or mounted on a 'selfie stick')
A friend, preferably a knowledgeable enthusiast
OBD2 code reader

A mirror, mounted at an angle on the end of a 'stick', in combination with a flashlight, can help you check the condition of the underside and sills of what is a low car. A borescope can peer down the back of the engine, or under the rear towards the diff and shafts, to check for leaks.

A phone camera, or digital camera lets you check details after you've left, you may notice details you missed at first glance. These photos are also nice memories, if you buy.

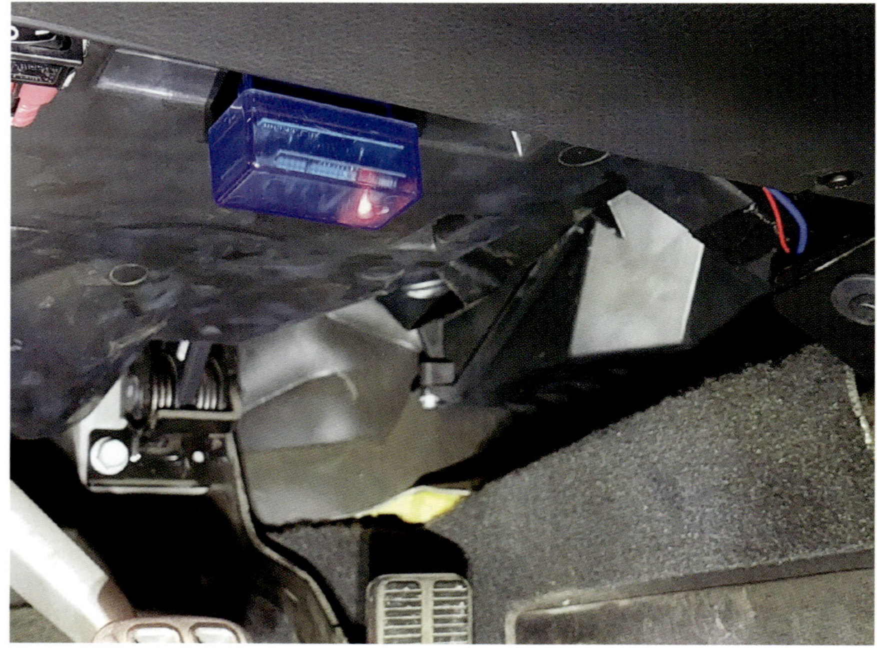

Bluetooth OBD plugged in to read trouble codes.

For those more used to an older car, you may be unfamiliar with, or nervous about, Onboard Diagnostics (OBD). Think of it as a way of the car telling you what is wrong with itself. You can purchase a simple code reader from as little as x10, some have their own handheld screen, others connect wirelessly to your mobile phone.

Generally, the more expensive the code reader, the more functions it can perform. With tech labor rates frequently exceeding x100 an hour, a code reader could pay for itself very quickly.

Ideally, have a friend or knowledgeable enthusiast accompany you: a second opinion is always valuable. A second pair of eyes may spot things you've missed.

7 Fifteen minute evaluation
– walk away or stay?

You will by now have asked the right questions of the seller by phone, social media or email and are feeling reasonably confident that this could be 'the one', provided the car is as described.

Your time is precious, as is that of the seller, so spend 15 minutes looking at the car and asking questions before you decide whether to invest more time, take it for a test drive, or agree to politely move on to the next car on your list.

The vendor
Remember, it's the car you're buying, not the seller. The appearance of the surroundings or your personal opinion of the seller, whilst factors to consider, are not proof of a good or bad car.

A pair of 2005-07 wireless keys. Missing a second trunk key.

Verification and keys
Check that the paperwork and keys are present; don't leave this to the end of your inspection. '05 to '07 C6s came with two key fobs and two separate emergency keys for the trunk. The fob design from 2008 had trunk keys integrated into the fobs.

Check that the chassis number (VIN) on the registration document matches those at the base of the windscreen and etched onto the inside vertical face of the front frame rail on the passenger side. With the hood open, look from the top, underneath the air filter (you may need to gently wipe this area clean then photograph it to be able to read the VIN).

Chassis VIN is hidden.

Body condition
C6 body panels are made of lightweight, impact resistant, rust-free, composite panels throughout. Dents are unusual, heavier impacts crack the body panel

and expose the fibrous material. Repairs are possible, though, using sheet moulded compound (SMC) or specific carbon fiber resin, fibers or filler.

Coupe, Convertible and Grand Sport models have front fenders and both bumper covers made from flexible RRIM (Reinforced Reaction Injection Molded) plastic. The other panels are SMC, not fiberglass as is commonly thought. The Z06 has front fenders and wheelhouses in carbon fiber composite, the CFZ carbon package added to that with carbon fiber front splitter, roof panel and rockers, whilst the ULZ Carbon Edition and ZR1 feature a raised carbon fiber hood, too. ZR1 has a clear window in the hood.

Impact damage behind door edge.

RRIM bumper that has just had a low-speed impact with a tree in Africa!

Using a flashlight, check the body panels for fine cracks (but not while it's raining). If the car is running wheel spacers or wider wheels, check whether the tires have made contact with the inner lip of the fenders.

Does the color match on each panel? Compare the panel gaps on each side, are they even?

Crouch down in front of the car and check for rock chips; the nose is low, and thus vulnerable to debris being thrown up from vehicles in front. Examine the front splitter on Z06 and ZR1 models, these are especially vulnerable to curb damage. Replacements start from x200 through to x2500 for genuine GM or carbon fiber.

Moisture in fog light.

Peer through the front grille with your flashlight: are the a/c condenser (from x50) and, if fitted, external oil cooler (from x500) damaged, have crumbling fins, or are they leaking?

C6 headlight covers are notorious for becoming cloudy or covered in microcracks. Usually, the lens covers require replacement (from x50 to x350 a pair). Usually, the lens covers require replacement (between x100 to x350 a pair), removed by heating them in the oven to 200F, just enough to soften the adhesive.

Amber running lights/turn signals run hot and can melt the sockets over time, making them lose contact. Replacement sockets are x10.

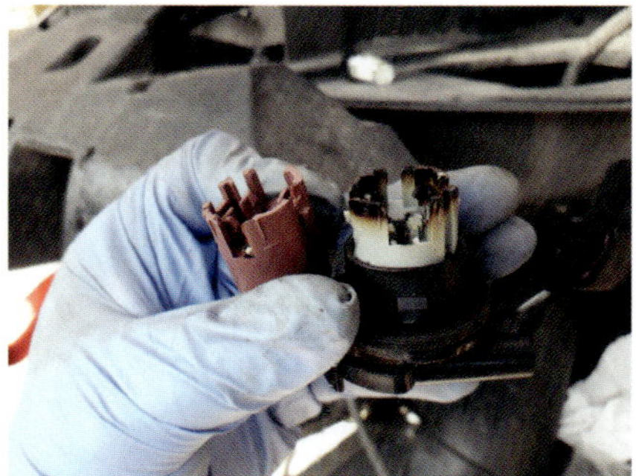

Old light socket showing signs of heat damage.

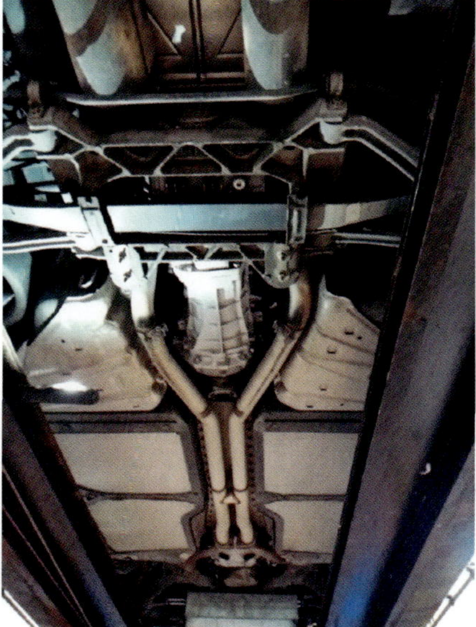

C6s have no undertrays, so access and visibility is good.

Crouch or lay down on each side of the car in turn and look at the condition of the underside of the rocker/sill covers. Incorrect jacking or grounding out over a high curb will damage these, and replacement is difficult as they are bonded to the chassis. The sill covers are at least only cosmetic, not structural. So, provided the metal chassis underneath is not dented, you'll need to decide if you can live with the cosmetic damage, perhaps using it as a bargaining point.

Most owners will use jacking pucks – either removable, or fixed in place in the frame rail slots.

Shine your flashlight forwards to the sump and check for oil dripping from this area. If there is, it could be a sump gasket, rear main seal or oil pressure sender. The sump gasket is best replaced by slightly lowering the subframe to remove and clean the sump and change the gasket. If you're unlucky and it's the rear main seal that's weeping through age, well, that's a 'torque tube and transmission out' job, involving hours of labor, and possibly other 'while you're in there' work, like a clutch replacement. The oil pressure sender is located behind the Corvette's plastic engine cover, in the passenger side bulkhead area. It's a cheap part to replace at ●x30, but access requires slender hands.

If you're looking at a Convertible, check the fabric hood carefully for frayed fabric or excessive chafing. Shiny areas of fabric are to be expected, and occur when the fabric rubs against itself as it's raised and lowered. A

Check fabric top for rubbing, note older C5 wheels on this car.

dye can be applied to faded fabric as a later fix.

Turn the steering to full lock and inspect the shocks for fluid leaks, especially on cars equipped with Magnetic Ride Control. Power steering leaks can come from a number of locations. The early, short, high-pressure hose has been revised for a longer design. Leaks from the rack sensor wires are difficult to cure, they are not a replaceable part and must be dried before resin or putty is applied. Steering rebuild and other specialists are listed in chapter 16.

Emergency key slot and car build codes on sticker.

Hatch/trunk

You can open the hatch (Coupe) or trunk (Convertible) in three convenient ways (if the engine is not running): from the key fob; a button to the lower left of the steering wheel; and by a hidden, rubber button above the rear licence plate (provided the key is on your person or close enough to the car). The rubber button can jam with road grime, but it's easily removed for cleaning.

There are two other methods: an emergency release handle inside the trunk; and a lock by the rear licence plate lights.

A Tech2, GM workshop tool.

Each key fob can have a different welcome message and convenience features programmed to it. Proximity sensors detect the key approaching the car, allowing you access without having to press any buttons. A word of warning: never open the trunk on the key button, slip it in a jacket pocket, throw it in the trunk and then close the lid! The proximity sensors can't detect the key there, leaving you locked out ... ask me how I know!

If the fob battery is flat, open the glovebox lid and insert the key into the slot within the glovebox. The car should recognise the key is present and allow it to start. Replace the CR2032 battery as soon as you can.

If the key fob is still not detected, it could be due to radio interference. Remove your mobile phone from the car, unplug everything from the 12v/USB sockets and try again. Alternatively, the remote control door lock receiver (RCDLR) could be the problem. No longer available new from GM, used modules can be checked for dry solder joints or a failed transistor. A refurbished or used module could be coded to your car using a GM Tech2, hand-held device.

If this is a Convertible with power top, check the hydraulic pump for fluid level and leaks. It's located in the passenger side of the trunk/tonneau cover, hidden behind the carpet. Unscrew by hand the single black plastic clip, fold down the carpet and use your flashlight. Rebuilt, uprated pumps are available from x600.

Hydraulic rams on each side should be strong enough to hold the lid in its highest position. If not, these are easily replaced, for x30 each.

Coupe models have power pull down on the hatch. Mind your fingers, but either lift and drop the hatch from a height of 12 inches (more effective with a door or window open), or gently push the hatch down and it will pull down. Convertibles don't have power pull down. Is the hatch/trunk lid flush with the surrounding body (and Coupe halo)? They can become misaligned if forced to close against an obstruction. Minor misalignment might be corrected by rotating the bump stops.

Under the hood

Pull the release handle in the driver's footwell and lift the hood in the area of the middle of the windshield cowl. Raise the hood to a vertical position, whereupon the hydraulic rams should keep it fully raised. If gravity does try to close the hood, budget for replacement struts at x65 for the pair.

Hood and hatch stay open on hydraulic rams. (Courtesy Joseph Perry)

All wet sump engines have a yellow-handled dipstick on the passenger side. Use the clean rag you brought along to check the oil level (if parked on level ground) and color. Dry sump engine oil levels should be checked after the test drive, described later.

Corvette C6s of all types have all-alloy engines. Use your magnet to check the engine block is non-magnetic. It's not unknown for an owner to have blown the original engine and replaced it with a cheaper, iron-block truck LS. These can be a way to produce strong power for a lower cost, but they add 100lb to the weight and should be declared in the advert.

Check the grey/black chassis tub lining on each side of the engine compartment for repairs.

Use your flashlight to look for leaks. Old rocker/valve cover gaskets can weep oil onto the exhaust headers on both sides of the V8. They are easy to change, at a cost of x20

Coolant leaks from hoses and the reverse side of the radiator can leave tell-tale stains, or drips underneath the car.

Check that all six steel exhaust manifold bolt heads are visible, on each side of the engine. The 10mm bolt heads have been known to pop off. Drilling out or welding nuts onto sheared studs is a time-consuming, risky business in situ. If long-tube headers are fitted (each branch of the exhaust manifold is individual, joining under the car), check the area carefully for heat damage. Specifically, look for damage to the clutch line (if a manual) on the driver's side firewall, and/or melted plastic connectors and wires. It is vital to shield or wrap the starter motor and clutch lines for reliable hot starting and avoiding fire when headers are fitted.

Leave the hood open for the tests to follow.

Unsupported, bowed radiator, due to cracked welds on radiator support.

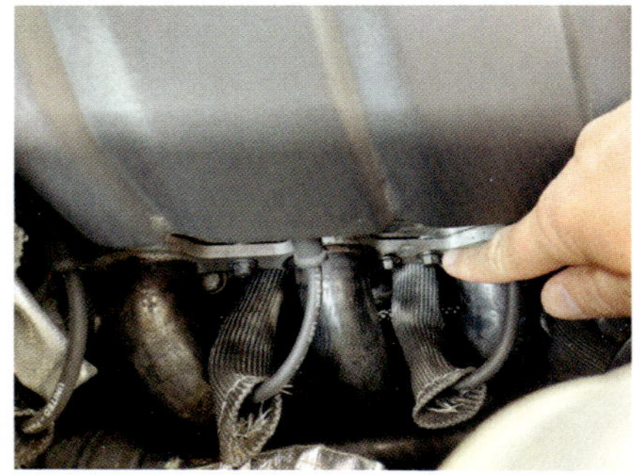

Header bolt heads can shear if over-tightened.

Interior

Open both doors in turn, by having one of the keys on your person and squeezing the black door touch pad. If the door is reluctant to open, needing a longer or firmer squeeze on the pad, they are an easy DIY job to clean contacts, or replace at ●x40. The windows should drop automatically by a small distance to clear the roof and frame. If a window snags, it probably just needs re-indexing, an easy process that takes seconds.

1. Close the door.
2. Raise the window by pulling up the switch.
3. Hold the up switch for three seconds after the window is closed. Release the switch.
4. Hold the up switch again for three seconds and release.

If one of the windows doesn't drop when opening a door, or makes a creaking noise, a window regulator probably requires replacement, at ●x350.

Fire it up!

Start the car ideally from cold, by depressing the clutch pedal (manual) or brake (auto) and pressing and releasing the top of the starter rocker switch.

The engine should fire into life quickly. All dials will perform a full sweep, welcome messages appear (you can change the name that appears) on the Digital

Start your engines.

Information Center (DIC) and warning lights will come on and (hopefully) go off. Units can be changed between US Imperial and Metric.

I've known of some owners who have managed to push the starter button through the dash! Usually this can be pushed back in place from the rear, but if not, a new switch is x60. Have your friend look out for blue smoke on startup, indicating valve stem/seal wear or piston ring blow-by? If on your own, it's worth having the owner start the car while you look for smoke from the exhausts. If this example is equipped with an NPP or Bi-mode exhaust, an initial loud bark will become quieter as vacuum builds and closes the exhaust actuators. The 'noisy', inner pair of tips will turn a darker color compared to the outer pair; this is normal and not a fault.

Press the trip button, to the right and behind the steering wheel, and scroll to the odo. Is the mileage as advertised? Further trip button presses reveal the % oil life remaining, but, given how easy this is to reset, it shouldn't be relied upon.

As the hood should still be open, the engine will be a little louder than you might expect, but there shouldn't be any nasty rattles or knocks. All LS engine lifters, rockers and injectors can sound a little like rattling sewing machines: amplified in cars with a modified camshaft or thin-walled headers. Lifters can fail, the giveaway being a loud, rythmic ticking noise that may change in tempo and volume as the engine warms. If caught early the cam may be unharmed, but a full set of lifters, including trays, for LS7 or quality alternatives, will be needed. Oil pressure is displayed on the top left gauge and also shown as a digital value, by cycling through the DIC menu, pressing the second button down, above trip.

Within a few seconds after starting from cold, the oil pressure should ideally be at least 30psi, with 40psi and higher more usual, depending on the engine, the oil used and the ambient temperatures. It is normal that as the oil warms, the pressure at idle will become lower. If it is pegged to maximum, it is usually a sign of a broken sender. Further button presses will show front and rear tire pressures, 30psi cold is normal, rising as the car is driven.

Voltage is shown top right, anywhere between 13.5 and 14.8 volts is considered normal when idling. A couple of tenths above or below that is acceptable for cars with a stock sized harmonic balancer pulley and stock alternator. An aftermarket 10% or 25% underdrive pulley may have slightly lower voltage.

The rev counter should settle at around 600rpm to 700rpm. This can vary if

An unmodified, narrow-bodied Coupe in a bright color still turns heads.

the car is fitted with a supercharger, or modified cam or tune.

Increase the fan blower speed and turn down the temperature. Turn on the A/C by pressing the button – you may hear a slight 'tick' as the compressor clutch engages. Check that the heated seats work while you wait for the AC to kick in. After a few minutes, cold air should come from the vents. A dirty cabin filter (changed under the hood) can introduce smells and cause the windows to steam.

A flashing climate screen indicates a fault. Sometimes this can happen intermittently for years, other times the climate head unit fails soon after. Disconnecting the battery negative for just a few seconds may help in the short term; fresh solder on any dry joints is the recognised fix. These climate head units are no longer available new, but used items are still easily found. Knightdrivetv.com makes a large 'Max-din' touch screen, that replaces both the climate and stereo units.

1LT climate control and stereo.

Convertible top

If the car is a Convertible, it's time to check the top operation. Ensure the car is in park (auto) or neutral (manual), the parking brake is engaged (you must be stationary), trunk closed and the windows are indexed.

Convertible top handle.

Manual top

Grip the handle above the interior mirror, lower and twist by 90 degrees: the windows will lower fully. Gently lift the first part of the fabric top nearest the windshield, you can return the handle back to the roof recess if you prefer. Get out the car, lift the rear section of the top, including glass window. Feel for a hidden button under the tonneau, behind the driver's side headrest. Press the button, lift the tonneau, lower the top fully, close the tonneau. It's an easy process and it takes just a few seconds once you've done it a few times.

Automatic top

Grip the handle above the interior mirror, lower and twist by 90 degrees, the windows will fully lower. The raise/lower rocker switch is in the dash, somewhat obscured by the left side of the steering wheel. Press and hold the lower part of the switch, the tonneau opens, the top folds back and the tonneau closes shut. When you hear a ding, it's finished. Release the button; it all happens in around 15 seconds.

During the operation, if the tonneau cover rubs against the rear window or top mechanism, there is an easy DIY fix, detailed in a Technical Service Bulletin (TSB). If the car is an 05 to 08, the rubbing is caused by the elastic straps stretching, replacements are ●x30. 08 onwards can be repaired by making a new hole in a strap, to increase clearance. Microswitches can fail or not quite make sufficient contact with the trunk or tonneau cover, resulting in 'top not secure' or other messages.

Seat covers fitted, therefore check the condition of the leather underneath.

8 Key points
– where to look for problems

Whilst most of these points are mentioned elsewhere, this chapter contains the most common, recognised C6 problems to consider. When presented with a list like this you could be forgiven to thinking these are unreliable cars. In reality, most cars will rarely experience any more than one or two issues.

Harmonic balancer

Every C6, regardless of model, year or mileage is likely to have (or has had) a problem with the original fit harmonic balancer. This is the main pulley on the front of the engine that takes the ancillary belts and minimizes damaging resonance and harmonics. They are multi-piece steel, with rubber bonding them together. Two problems occur, firstly, the stretch bolt can back out and rub against the steering rack, damaging the thread on the end of the crank. The more common occurrence is a wobble and chirping noise where the rubber starts to oscillate and separate from the inner and outer steel parts; worst case they completely detach. It is all too easy to develop wobble paranoia, with groups and forums full of owners posting videos of their pulleys and asking, "Is this a normal amount of movement?"

Even when the cars were new from the factory, it was common to have a small

Removing original harmonic balancer, note 6.0L marking, usually hidden behind water pump.

amount of oscillation. This is a topic to really divide opinion, but if the belt isn't chirping when the engine idles, the tensioner isn't bouncing dramatically, and the pulley has no more than 1/8in of movement, you are probably fine at the present time.

If a replacement is required, don't use an OEM style, cheap pulley. Instead opt for a Powerbond 'Race', ATI or other quality unit, with new stretch bolt or multi-use ARP bolt. This would also be a good time to change belts, tensioners, front cover plate seal, crank seal, water pump, and possibly the oil pump, sprockets and chain. Perhaps the perfect excuse to fit a performance camshaft, too?

Diagnostic codes

The OBD2 socket is located underneath the steering column, set into a plastic cover (see photo on page 26). Plug in the code reader, press the top of the start button to the 'run' position (feet off the pedals), or start the engine, then read the codes. Make a note of any that appear, search for them online, then reset them to see if they reappear on the test drive.

Automatic issues

Automatics from all years can become stuck in park, usually due to a failed/failing park lockout solenoid (shift interlock system), or the park switch not fully closing. Whilst common, this is thankfully something that can be DIY fixed, preferably before it happens at the wrong time. Shift cables can break (x40), but usually it is the plastic bushing/grommet that fails at either end (5 and an hour or two DIY), diagnosed by the shifter moving forwards and back with no resistance.

Fuel smells?

Do you smell gasoline from the driver's side area? On 07 to 13 models, the driver's side plastic fuel pump sender unit can crack, leading to a strong fuel smell and possible leaks when the tank is over half full. There was no recall, and the 10 year/120,000 mile GM goodwill period TSB has ended. 05 and 06 models are not immune from this, but the metal plate is stronger. O rings on the crossover pipe between the pair of fuel tanks have occasionally leaked. Evidence of a prior repair to the fuel system should be considered a positive, as work in this area can require significant hours to rectify. The EVAP solenoids can fail, throwing a DIC error code but these are an easy and cheap DIY replacement.

Steering issues

05 is the only year where a steering column lock is fitted. A carry over from the C5, these units can fail, locking the steering in one place, with a 'service column lock' warning on the DIC. A bypass eliminator is available for x70. A TSB describes how a dealer can remove the locking ring and reprogram the BCM as a permanent fix.

Engine issues

The 427 cubic inch/7-liter LS7 fitted to the Z06 and 427 makes big power, but has two, well reported problems: valve/head issues and titanium rod coatings. These issues can affect all model years, with mileage and use not necessarily a factor. You will not be able to easily check for these issues during a typical pre-purchase inspection, but it's important to be aware of them.

Adverts for Z06 will frequently list if the stock heads have been 'fixed', or

LS7 is an awesome engine, despite a couple of known issues.

aftermarket heads have been installed and by whom. Valve guides wear on the LS7, with the titanium valves losing their Chromium Nitride coating. The valve stem thins and ultimately breaks from the valve head, causing carnage when the piston meets the broken valve head. To help diagnose the amount of valve and guide wear, there is a procedure known as the wiggle test, for measuring lateral play. This is performed with the valve covers, rockers, retainers and springs removed.

The LS7 has lightweight, titanium connecting rods with a Chromium Nitride coating. This coating has been know to wear through, causing the shoulders of the rods to rub together, adding abrasive titanium particles to the oil, rapidly wearing moving parts and reducing oil pressure. Thankfully, this issue is not common, and is more usually seen in those cars driven hard and regularly on track. LS9 rods don't suffer from this problem.

LS9 engines are exceptionally strong, but if you start upping boost or driving hard, the stock intercooler 'bricks' can develop pin hole leaks. Parts of the top and bottom alloy plates can break up, too. Before damage to engine and supercharger occurs, upgraded bricks are recommended, from C&R or Kong, from x1200.

Front ends are low, obviously, and rubber air dams *will* scrape on the ground. This is normal, but check for broken radiator support welds and excessive damage to the front bumper cover. Sill covers become damaged through incorrect jacking.

Radiator supports scrape the pavement and can crack.

A very worn corner air dam piece, compared to new.

Interiors

Seats can sag when the foam starts to poke through the frame base. Leather can crack in high mileage cars and those that get cooked in the sun. Rebuild kits are available.

Leather dash coverings on the highest trim levels frequently shrink and lift. A good quality repair is difficult and best left to a professional. Aftermarket leather covers are available to be glued in place, should the original become too damaged.

This headlight lens needs to be replaced.

Headlights

Headlight lenses become cloudy and microcracked.

Exhausts

NPP and Bi-mode exhaust valves can rattle, and internal baffles can crack. Valves are unavailable from GM, but Porsche 997s use the same part (#99711168000). Should they vibrate at idle, the boxes can be cut open, repaired and welded back together. Whilst making this repair, Z06 perforated inner tubes can be covered, to increase volume when in loud mode.

Rattles from NPP exhausts are easily repaired.

9 Serious evaluation

– 60 minutes for years of enjoyment

Score each section using the boxes as follows:
4 = Excellent; 3 = good; 2 = average; 1 = poor. The totting up procedure is detailed at the end of the chapter. Be realistic in your marking!

If, after appraising a car for 15 minutes you feel that it's not the right one for you, be polite and walk away. Hopefully, though, things are looking good enough to continue the inspection.

Engine

Given that LS engines can be swapped between models, it's worth establishing that the one fitted is what you expect. The engine casting numbers are difficult to access in a C6 without a borescope, as they are hidden behind components. The head type number is easy to see on the front passenger side, and etched numbers may be found on the block, although these usually refer to an internal reference or build date. 243 refers to LS2 heads, 821 to LS3, 8452 to LS7.

243 indicate LS2 heads.

Timing chain tensioners

These can break, although this is rare and can go undetected until parts are discovered in the sump or blocking the oil pressure sender. The stronger LS2 'dogbone' tensioner is usually retrofitted in this case. Score 4 if this has been done; 3 if not.

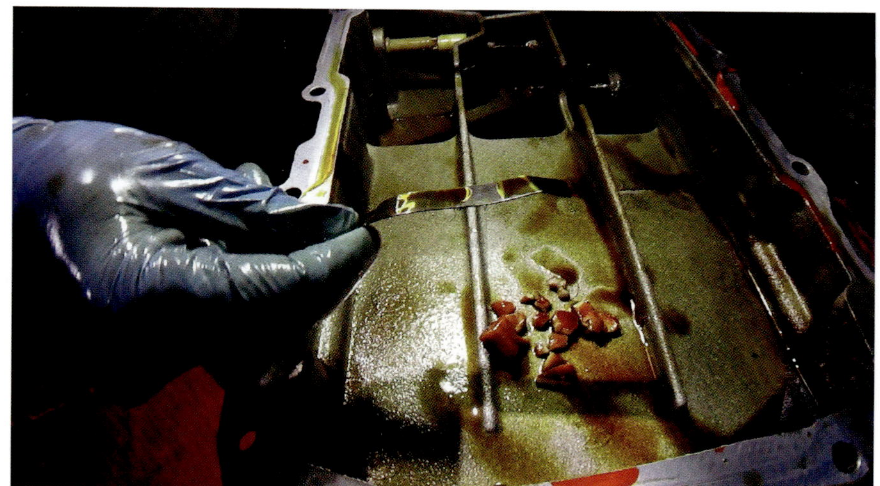

These parts of the chain tensioner dropped into the sump without harm!

Replacing original, yellow, LS2 valve springs.

Rocker arm bearings    

Needle bearings can fall out of rocker arms, particularly on cars with an uprated cam and stronger valve springs. Sometimes this only comes to light when an owner discovers a needle or two stuck to the magnetic sump plug or in the oil pan. A trunion upgrade kit with caged bearings is from x150. Score 4 if this has been done; 3 if not.

Clutch

On manual cars it is perfectly normal for the clutch fluid to look black. Even fresh fluid will turn dark within a few hundred miles. Unless an aftermarket remote bleeder has been fitted, the only practical way of flushing the clutch fluid is by sucking a small amount of fluid out of the filler, using a baster or syringe, and topping up with fresh brake fluid. Pump the clutch multiple times and repeat the process above, until the fluid is clear.

If it is a manual car, depress the clutch; some owners report that the feel is heavy. This may not indicate an issue, just a characteristic of that car or the clutch fitted. The clutch pedal itself has a return assist spring; in some cases this falls off, being found on the driver's side carpet, with no adverse effects. Score 1 if the clutch needs replacement; 4 if it feels good on the test drive.

Engine mounts

These are fluid-filled and they will perish and leak with age. It can be very difficult to observe this by feel, occasionally tell-tale leaks can be seen (it's quite easy and cost-effective to change them). Score 4 if recently replaced; 3 if visibly leaking.

An engine mount at 200k miles

Front underside

Crouch down at the front of the car, you may be able to see the alloy lower radiator support. These are painted black, with alloy exposed from scraping. Welds crack, ultimately leading to leaks from the unsupported radiator. Whilst the support can be removed and repaired, it is more usual to replace it, either for a cheap copy or a higher quality example from a company like Crane's Corvette.

Underneath the front bumper cover should be a three-piece, full-width rubber air dam. These are important for cooling at higher speeds, by directing air into the radiators and by creating an air pressure differential. Are they present? Don't be surprised to see them scraped and worn down, they are sacrificial and therefore made of rubber for a reason. Reproduction parts cost from x100, for all three parts. Score 4 if all pieces pieces of front airdam are present and in good condition; 3 if not.

Part of the rubber air dam is missing.

Lights and body

C7 and C8 style LED headlights and LED taillamps give a fresh look, available from companies like Morimoto, as well as cheaper Chinese outlets. Prices and quality vary wildly, just check they work. Score 4 if the headlight lenses are clear, 2 if they are cloudy or cracked.

Badges

The vibrant colors in the self-adhesive factory badges fade in sunlight. They can be removed using fishing line and adhesive remover. New genuine GM 'waterfall' badges are x150 for front (curved) and x80 rear, with replicas from eBay from x20. Both will fade again in time. Score according to condition.

LED lamps give a fresh look.

Sun-faded front badge.

General bodywork

It is normal for small rocks to accumulate between the rear quarters and sill covers, in front of the rear tires, by the GM logos fitted between 2006 and early 2010.

ZR1 hood windows can become cloudy, scratched and detached from the hood. Now discontinued from GM, copies are of mixed quality, so restoring the original window may be preferable. It can be bonded back in place with fresh adhesive.

A perfect condition ZR1 hood window.

When these clips break, the bumper cover lifts.

Some aftermarket rear spoilers are 'no drill' affixed by adhesive tape in places; these can lift at the edges.

The edges of the front bumper cover commonly lift where they meet the headlight, when one or both plastic clips on each side are broken. Whilst care must be taken, these clips can be replaced for less than x10, without needing to remove the bumper cover. Score according to overall condition.

Wheels

All C6s had staggered sizes, with the front wheels one inch smaller diameter than the rear (18/19 on narrow body, 19/20 inch on wide body). Rear tires are also wider than fronts. As you travel around the car look at each wheel in turn. Are the alloy wheels corroded or curbed? If so, allow a cost of around x80 per wheel for refurbishment or repair. If missing, genuine center caps are between x25 and x70 each.

Stock alloy wheels of all styles are generally strong and not overly heavy. Twin spoke Speedline alloys, as fitted to early year Z06, had a few reported cases of spokes cracking, but this is unusual.

Aftermarket reproduction alloys, are heavier than the originals and can be weaker.

Salt can pit the finish of chrome and they're more challenging and expensive to refurbish, compared to a painted or polished finish.

All Corvette C6 alloys have 5 x 120.65mm (4.75 inches) stud pattern. Wheels for BMWs are a very close fitment, at 5 x 120, but present a risk, with higher load

Corvette C6s deserve quality tires.

placed on the wheel studs. If wheel spacers are fitted, they should be quality, hubcentric (centered and supported on the hub and wheel bore), with lugnuts having at least eight threads of engagement.

Grand Sport and Z06 wheels fitted to a narrow body car, stick out from the body and usually results in cracked fenders.

Are locking lug nuts fitted (one on each wheel)? If so, ask to see the locking wheel nut key, and check it fits.

Score wheels according to overall condition.

Tires

Tires should match, be of a quality brand and have deep tread. Check the sidewalls for cracking, gouges, and for the date of manufacture. Mismatched or cheap tires may give an indication an owner or garage is prepared to skimp in other areas. Uneven tread wear could be down to a number of factors, such as poorly maintained tire pressures, an alignment set-up is needed, subframe could have been out of alignment when tightened, worn rubber suspension bushes (Poly, Delrin, Spherical upgrades available), play in ball joints, track driving (eccentric adjusters can slip), or possible frame damage. Each tire could cost anywhere between x160 and x500 depending on the size, brand and performance. Score according to overall condition.

Brakes

Brake pads and rotors should be inspected. It's normal for rear rotors to have

Spacers are best used with extended studs. Cadillac ATS Brembo calipers.

Drilled rotor with crack and a lip, showing wear.

an unswept portion on Coupe and Convertible. Electronic pad wear sensors were only fitted to those models with carbon ceramic rotors. All others had a simple metal tab that created a screeching noise against the rotor, to let you know they are getting low. Z06 and Grand Sport have 'padlets', small, individual pads within each caliper. Z51/ J55 drilled rotors can crack from the holes. Heavily lipped, or scored discs should be replaced rather than re-faced.

Carbon Ceramic rotors, as used on the ZR1 and some Z06 don't wear in the same way as iron, they simply reduce in density/weight as they become hot and worn. Removing and weighing these is not going to be possible pre-purchase,

Carbon ceramics are expensive, but effective at resting fade.

so establishing if/when they were last replaced could be useful. Check each carbon ceramic rotor carefully around the outer edge, they can be easily damaged when mounting wheels or contacting the ground. Carbon ceramic rotors are long lasting but expensive, costing as much as x2000 per rotor, or less for refurbishment. A quality, two-piece iron rotor conversion is sometimes chosen instead. Score 4 for rotors and pads in good condition; 2 for heavily worn or damaged rotors and pads.

Interior

Stereo system

The factory stereo is best described as adequate, the upgraded BOSE system is slightly better, therefore upgrades are common, both to speakers and to a newer, aftermarket Double Din touch screen system.

OnStar was a now defunct, US only GM service. Any remaining parts for this can be removed, but you will lose handsfree Bluetooth calling if still using the factory stereo. For those in North America, Sirius XM Satellite radio equipment was optional up to 08, then standard on all model years after this, provided an annual subscription is paid.

Sat Nav is showing its age.

Mirrors

Look up, if this car is a higher trim level it will have an auto-dimming mirror function. Press the power button to see if it dims, or becomes clearer. Is the mirror glass free of streaks or yellowing? If not, a replacement costs between x175 and x500, depending on the part number. If it isn't operating at all, check the fuse and cable

Illumination of these HUD buttons can fail: dry solder or bulbs?

plugging into the back of the mirror. A specialist like radar-mirror.com may be able to repair the original for less. Score 2 if an auto-dipping mirror is present but needs replacement; 4 if it functions.

Glass

The dash top creates reflection and glare on the inside of the windshield. It can be reduced or eliminated by wearing polarized sunglasses, cleaning with a matt spray, covering with a dash pad, flocking or Alcantara material.

Look for large or small cracks in the front windshield. Being low cars, they can end up covered in tiny chips over time. Shining your flashlight from the outside may help you see them. The factory dimples at the top of the Coupe rear screen make it more difficult for a window tint film to adhere to. Dark tints, if no longer wanted, can be removed with heat.

Cars equipped with HUD will project a green display onto the bottom of the windshield, this can only be seen from a driver's seated position. Using the additional set of buttons, behind the left side of the steering wheel, the + button will increase the brightness and the ∧ or v buttons moves the display up or down. If you can't see anything on the windshield, the HUD tilt mirror pivot could be broken, or fuse 15 blown. Try looking through the windshield, from outside the car, to look for a green glow in the dash top window.

Cars with HUD had a specific glass with DuPont 'Wedge' interlayer, to enhance the effectiveness of the projected display. HUD also works just fine on regular windshield glass. Replacement HUD glass can produce a ghosting/double, either

A very nice interior. Note the aftermarket dash top pad added to eliminate reflection.

of the HUD display or oncoming car lights during darkness. Score 2 if HUD is not functioning; 4 if it is.

Head-up display (HUD) window.

Furniture

4 3 2 1

Interiors generally wear well; cars with over 200,000 miles can be in better condition than those from other manufacturers with a quarter of that. Check the wear to the steering wheel, driver's seat bolster and base to give clues as to the mileage of the car. Low mileage cars with excessive wear should ring alarm bells. Glovebox latches can break, these are available online for ●x20.

Mileage

Mileage is stored in both the Electronic Control Module (ECM) and Instrument Control Panel (ICP), but it is possible for the unscrupulous to tamper with both. This is where a history check is vital, as well as what your eyes tell you as to the condition of the car.

Carpets

Lift the floor mats (if fitted), check the carpet condition underneath. Check the interior carpet for stains or damage. Lift up any trunk liner to reveal any damage to the tub, if any acoustic mat has been added, or any mounting holes that could have been used for a speaker box or even nitrous. Is the black underside of the lid badly scratched? Some Coupes, from 2LT trim upwards came with a luggage shade and cargo net; is it present? Score according to condition.

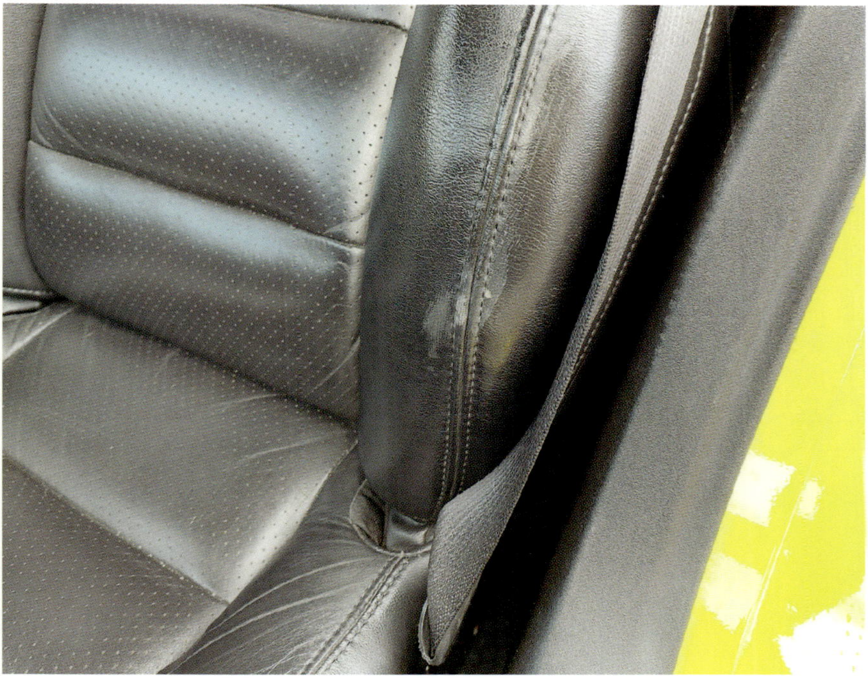

Light wear to seat bolster.

Test drive

This is the most important part of the serious evaluation stage and one you have probably been most looking forward to.

Warming up

4 3 2 1

Engine coolant warms quicker than oil, so wait for the oil to reach at least 150ºF (approximately 10 to 15 minutes of steady driving) before using the full performance of the car. From the factory, models with an external oil cooler (such as Z06) didn't come with an oil thermostat. In cold climes this can lead to a very slow oil temperature rise, therefore a quality thermostat (such as from Improved Racing) is recommended.

Suspension

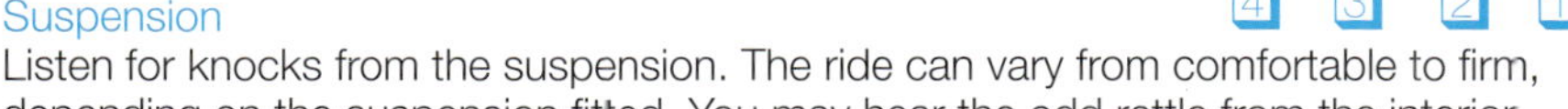

4 3 2 1

Listen for knocks from the suspension. The ride can vary from comfortable to firm, depending on the suspension fitted. You may hear the odd rattle from the interior trim or targa roof, but knocking sounds are not normal.

Knocking or thumping could be anti-roll bar links, ball joints or suspension bushes, it will be hard to tell which. It only takes a small amount of play to make a big noise. If Magnetic Ride Control is fitted, switch between tour and sport modes whilst driving, the change is noticeable and instant.

Is the car pulling to either side when accelerating or braking? Is the steering wheel lined up straight when you are driving straight? Tramlining could be easily

You'll love the way a C6 drives. (Courtesy Joseph Perry)

6

rectified with four-wheel tracking (alignment), or replacing tired suspension components. If Magnetic Ride Control is present but not working or leaking score 1; 4 if it switches between modes correctly on the test drive.

Knocking from the suspension scores 2, or 4 if the suspension has no unusual noises and the alignment is straight.

Brakes    

On a clear stretch of road, brake firmly but not so hard as to trigger the ABS. The car may pull slightly to one side if the road is cambered, but should reduce speed without drama or shaking. Any banging or dramatic veering to either side is a cause for concern. Stock brakes on all models should feel strong, although they do require a firmer pedal press compared to many over-assisted modern cars. If they are underwhelming, the brake pads or fluid could be old. Any wobbling or pulsing through the pedal may be due to pad material that has transferred to the rotor (it is rarely a warped rotor); this may improve through the course of the test drive. Drilled rotors with cracks that reach the outside edge will result in a very noticeable, rhythmic vibration through the car when braking. Score according to condition and function.

Traction    

The traction and stability controls are effective at countering excessive wheelspin or sliding but they can't beat physics, of course. Sometimes the traction control is just a little too intrusive, so pressing the active handling button once will allow wheelslip, whilst still leaving the active handling on. A second press will enter Competitive

Best saved for after you have bought the car.

Traction and stability control button.

Driving mode, allowing a greater degree of slip, before the active handling reigns in a slide. A long press and hold will turn off all safety systems, except the anti-lock brakes, which will always remain on. A short press of the same button switches the safety systems back on. ZR1s from 2010 have a more sophisticated five-stage performance traction management.

Service Active Handling errors on the DIC are usually caused by the steering position sensor or loose wiring at the sensor plug. The sensor itself is x40; changing it involves working inside the cabin, removing the airbag and other parts. On very rare occasions, an active handling error could result in the car applying individual brakes, in the mistaken belief the car is skidding, even with active handling and traction control switched off on the button. Score 4 for no DIC handling errors, 3 for the 'service active handling' message.

Differential

All C6 models have plate-type limited-slip differentials (Positraction). In time, the clutch packs and pre-load washers will naturally wear, with the result that an inside wheel will spin when accelerating out of a tight junction. Manual models from 2010 onwards have launch control.

You may notice a popping or grumbling noise from the front or back end when turning tightly at slow speeds, in forwards or reverse. The noise at the front is the tires scrubbing and jumping over the pavement, and is nothing to worry about: it is a result of wide front tires and Ackerman angle. This sort of noise from the rear is either the differential and/or hub nuts. Changing to the correct AC Delco LS differential fluid and performing slow figure of eights to work in the new fluid will help. Old hub nuts can either be correctly torqued or better still, removed, the threads cleaned of rust, with new nuts fitted (x10 each) and correctly torqued. Popping or grumbling from the rear when turning at low speeds scores 3; a silent rear end scores 4.

Rust on the hub splines can cause a popping noise when turning.

Roof

Plenty of Coupe and Grand Sport owners have joined the 'flying roof club', placing their removable targa panel in place, then driving off before latching (tell yourself never to do this)! If the optional translucent roof is fitted, look for cosmetic microcracking in the top layer of Lexan. Melrose T Tops can replace the acrylic onto your original roof frame for x895.

The Convertible roof (if raised) should feel snug, with no gaps to let in drafts or leaks.

All other models, whether fixed roof or targa, should have minimal creaks. Roof panel noises can be cured by replacing or softening weather stripping, torquing and covering locating pins and applying grease. With targa panel removed/Convertible top down, buffeting is minimal at legal speeds, with Convertibles subjectively having slightly smoother airflow around the cabin. Score 4 for a snug, good condition roof; 3 if lightly damaged, creaking or drafty.

Raise the roof on the test drive, to check for drafts.

Steering

Every Corvette C6 has hydraulic power steering; this was slightly revised for 2008, with a variable ratio rack with all-new internals fitted from 2009. All except the non-Z51 Coupe and Convertible have a simple, finned fluid cooler. Score 2 if power steering is leaking or excessively noisy when turning; 4 if not.

Signals

Are the turn signals 'hyper-flashing'? Changing incandescent bulbs for LEDs will require the addition of securely mounted resistors in parallel, to avoid the Body Control Module (BCM) thinking a bulb is broken and flashing the remaining bulbs too quickly. Specialists such as Sharplightinnovations.com (see chapter 16) has an excellent range of led solutions, including products useful to those wishing to convert lighting to European standards. Score 3 if turn signals are hyper-flashing; 4 if not.

Heat soak

It is normal to feel some warmth through the carpet covering the center tunnel, particularly on a summer's day. Kits are available to reduce this if needed.

With a standard thermostat, the coolant will typically run between 190F and 220F. In hot weather, as high as 230F (255F maximum) is acceptable, but does the temperature drop again with steady driving? If not, the fan plug (passenger side, behind radiator shroud) could have melted. These can be replaced, or some owners bypass the connector, hard wiring them. As on all cars, the air conditioning condenser will accumulate road debris. This can be blown, or washed out from the rear, to improve airflow.

Gearchange

Manual

The manual gearshift on all model years has a long throw, compared to the short, rifle bolt action in a Mazda or Honda, but you should find you can select all six gears positively, even from cold. Aftermarket, short-throw shifters are popular additions. Reverse is locked out if you are moving forwards, so you don't need to worry about accidentally pushing too far to the right in normal manoeuvring. To select reverse, it's just a case of being stationary, pushing firmly to the right and forwards.

Computer Aided Gear Selection (CAGS) guided the gear lever from 1st to 4th at low speeds, to help with emissions controls. It is fortunately easily and cheaply overcome with a small harness added above the gearbox, for as little as x10. Most cars already have this fitted.

Automatics

If you are driving a 2005 automatic, you will be using Drive (D). When you come to a stop, slide the lever down, to '1'. When you pull away it will keep the gear in 1st, until you are ready to change up, by selecting 2nd and so on. It gives you a form of control over what the gearbox is doing, by preventing it from changing beyond the selected ratio.

Using the paddle shift can be fun

A 2006 and newer model has a six-speed automatic gearbox, with manual control on both the shifter buttons on the steering wheel. Start off driving in D, then slide the lever to the bottom, into S, where the gearbox will hold onto each ratio for longer.

Using either thumb, press either + button, situated each side of the steering wheel spokes, to change up a gear. Each press selects another gear. To downshift, pull either button towards you. To return to full auto mode, slide the shifter from S, back to D. For those more used to the industry standard 'pull right paddle to change up, pull left paddle to change down' a simple wire switch or splice at the shifters achieves this. For those who don't want to modify wiring, an F1 paddle shift module is available for x170. Larger shifter paddles can be bought at extra cost.

Automatic shifts should be smooth, vibration free and, whilst not instantaneous, reasonably quick.

Rubber giubo couplings can fail, particularly with repeated hard launches.

Torque tube

Both manual and auto cars should have barely detectable noise from the transmission. The driveshaft runs within a rigid torque tube, down the center of the underside. At each end are rubber couplings (giubos) and bearings. With high miles, high power or repeated aggressive launches at the drag strip, these can become damaged or worn. Being a rotating part that is several feet long, noises from this area can be difficult to locate, or differentiate from clutch/flywheel. A marble in a can or rattle noise that changes at different revs or idle 'could' be from the torque tube. To get to this area involves removing the rear-mounted differential and gearbox, so typically leads to quite a few 'while you're in there' jobs, including the clutch, remote bleeder and rear main seal, if still original. Suspected torque tube or transmission noise scores 1 star; no noise, especially with evidence of torque tube and clutch work is 4 .

Higher speeds

On a suitable road and with the engine fully warmed up, run the engine to higher speeds, through the gears, listening for misfire, clutch slip, hesitation or unwillingness to rev. Popular opinion says that oil pressure should be at least 10psi per 1000rpm, although the workshop manual states a lower tolerance of 24psi at 4000rpm and 212F oil temperature.

Depending on the model of LS engine fitted, they deliver their maximum power between 5900rpm and 6500rpm and can be safely accelerated to their rev limiters beyond this.

When accelerating hard, look in the mirrors to check for smoke. In the unlikely event you do see a small puff of smoke on a full throttle gear change, the addition of an oil catch can may help. Larger plumes of blue smoke on the overrun are probably worn valve stem seals or piston rings, but are typically only a problem on very high mileage cars or those with forced induction added.

Loose windshield cowls (black plastic beneath the wipers) can vibrate and buzz, making a surprising amount of noise at speed (typically 70mph+). A DIY cure involves double-sided foam tape, or silicone, under the mounting tabs.

Low oil pressure or blue smoke is 0; good oil pressure and no smoke 4.

After the test drive

At the end of the test drive, press the bottom of the start/stop button to stop the engine. Press the lock/unlock button on the door, followed by the circular button on the door handle to leave the car. For security, when away from the Corvette, keep your keys in a Faraday pouch (signal blocker) to lessen the chance of theft.

After a minute, it is good practice to re-start the car, to confirm that it will start when hot.

Between 5 and 20 minutes after stopping the warm engine, you should check the oil level on dry-sumped cars. The tank is located by the passenger side bulkhead; the dipstick has a yellow handle.

Evaluation procedure

Add up the total points.

Score: 120 = excellent; 90 = good; 60 = average; 30 = poor. Cars scoring over 84 will be completely usable and will require only maintenance and care to preserve condition. Cars scoring between 30 and 61 will require some serious work (at much the same cost regardless of score). Cars scoring between 62 and 83 will require very careful assessment of the necessary repair/restoration costs in order to arrive at a realistic value.

10 Auctions

– sold! Another way to buy your dream

Pros: Prices will usually be lower than dealers or private sellers, and you might grab a real bargain on the day. Auctioneers have usually established clear title with the seller. You can bid at most auctions from the comfort of your own home. You don't have to haggle a price as there's no salesperson to haggle with, the final bid plus fees is what you pay.
Cons: You have to rely on a description of condition and history, if you can't get to view the car yourself. The opportunity to inspect at the auction is limited, and the biggest drawback is you cannot drive the car. Auction cars are often a little below par and may require some work. The estimate is often priced unrealistically low, and it's easy to overpay if you get carried away by 'auction fever'. You may have less protection should the car have faults, particularly when descriptions of faults are generic. Accident damaged, stolen recovered, repossessed, flood cars and lemons are more likely to appear through an auction. Factor in transport costs for non-driving cars, or those located a long distance away.

Trade auctions

Some auction companies are trade only and require an account. It's becoming increasingly common for auction companies to dress or improve damaged cars in photos.

Check for damage on auction cars.

Catalogue, entry fee and payment details

When you purchase the catalogue of the vehicles in a more traditional auction, it often acts as a ticket allowing two people to attend the viewing days and the auction. The catalogue will contain a brief description of the car, guide price, buyer's premium, and details of acceptable forms of payment. At the fall of the hammer an immediate deposit is usually required, the balance payable within 24 hours. There are sometimes payment restrictions, so find out the auction's accepted method. No car will be released before all payments are cleared, don't forget the buyer's premium and any additional local taxes.

Viewing

In some instances it's possible to view. A test drive however is highly unlikely.

Bidding

Before you take part in the auction, decide your maximum bid – and stick to it! Assuming that you are the successful bidder, the auctioneer will note your card or paddle number, and from that moment on you will be responsible for the vehicle.

If the car is unsold, either because it failed to reach the reserve or because there was little interest, it may be possible to negotiate with the owner, via the auctioneers, after the sale is over.

Insert T hooks into the sill slots, under any jacking puck that may be fitted.

Successful bid

There are two more things to consider: how to get the car home, and insurance. Come equipped for all eventualities, such as rope, tools, jump pack, fluids, jack, long boards. European C6s have a removable towing eye that screws into the front bumper.

US cars don't have any easy provision for towing onto a trailer. Recovery companies with a flatbed truck will use a V Bridle with T hooks (Amazon has these from x50), that locate into the jacking points behind the front wheels, pulling the Corvette onto long boards, to lessen the chance of the front scraping. Some owners report pulling from the lower front wishbones without damage.

Track cars may have been equipped with permanent towing points, from companies such as vorshlag-store.com.

Auctioneers

Barrett-Jackson www.barrett-jackson.com/
Bonhams www.bonhams.com/
British Car Auctions (BCA) www.bca-europe.com or www.british-car-auctions.co.uk/
Cheffins www.cheffins.co.uk/
Christies www.christies.com/
Copart www.copart.com/
Coys www.coys.co.uk/
ebay www.ebay.com/
H&H www.classic-auctions.co.uk/
RM www.rmauctions.com/
Shannons www.shannons.com.au/
Silver www.silverauctions.com

11 Paperwork

– correct documentation is essential!

The paper trail

The best C6 should ideally come with a large portfolio of paperwork, accumulated and passed on by a succession of proud owners. This documentation represents the real history of the car. From it, can be deduced the level of care the car has received, how much it's been used, which specialists have worked on it, and the dates of major repairs, parts fitted and restorations. Window stickers and build sheets are available to purchase from the National Corvette Museum, should the originals have been lost.

Service history

C6s sold in the US don't come with a printed service book for collecting dealer stamps; service records are recorded electronically by GM. A VIS record can be requested from a GM service dealership. A Carfax report may also show service records.

Self-servicing

If the car has been serviced at home by an enthusiastic (and hopefully capable) owner, try to obtain as much service history, receipts and other paperwork pertaining to the car as you can.

Photos of self-servicing, as well as receipts are valuable.

Registration documents

It is essential to check that the registration document is genuine, that it relates to the car in question, and that all the seller and vehicle details are correctly recorded, including chassis/VIN and engine numbers (if these are shown). Ensure the title is correctly transferred to you.

Roadworthiness certificate

Most country/state administrations require that vehicles are regularly tested to prove they are safe to use on the public highway and do not produce excessive emissions. In the UK, that test (the 'MoT') is carried out every year at approved testing stations, for a fee. In the USA, the requirement varies, but many states insist on an emissions test every two years as a minimum, while the police are charged with pulling over unsafe-looking vehicles. If you are from a State where a smog test is required, it is worth checking if catalytic convertors are fitted and if the car has had a tune.

Road licence

Whatever form of 'road license/tax' is required in your home area, it must relate to the vehicle carrying it, and must be present and valid if the car is to be legally driven

Is the license plate still valid?

on the public highway. The value of the license will depend on the length of time it will continue to be valid.

Some US states apply a 'tax' on the annual registration/license plate fee, others are based on the value or year of the car.

In the UK, it is vital to know that the moment ownership (responsibility to pay tax) is transferred to a new keeper, you must tax the car before driving it away.

HPI/Carfax hidden history

Many cars are reputed to have had a hidden past, such as having been written off/total loss, stolen/recovered, had a change of registration number, or still have finance owing. If buying privately, you should always carry out a check via Carfax, carVertical, HPI or similar. If buying from a dealership, it should have already checked for this, so ask for a copy of this certificate, for both peace of mind and guarantee. Plenty of accident repairs go unrecorded, so you still need to check a car carefully, even if it has no adverse history. Be particularly aware of imported cars, where a title may not be recorded, such as those coming from the middle east.

Online investigation

A bit of sleuthing online can sometimes reveal more. C6 owners are often enthusiasts who frequent forums and social media groups. Posts and write-ups from the current or previous owners, even photos and videos, help build a picture of the car and its treatment.

Carbon-bodied drift C6, with Mazda rotary power.

12 What's it worth?

– let your head rule your heart

Condition

If you used the marking system in chapter 9 you'll know whether the car is in Excellent (maybe Concours), Good, Average or Poor condition or, perhaps, somewhere in between these categories.

Trade and consumer price guides exist, although they seem more accurate for mainstream cars rather than sports cars, sometimes undervaluing C6s. Prices for Corvette C6s in the States rose sharply during the Covid pandemic, then dropped down a little and now seem relatively stable as the market appreciates these modern classics. Collectors' models, for example, low-mileage ZR1s, have seen prices rising. In Europe, perhaps due to high taxes and gas prices, combined with low numbers, asking prices remain strong.

ZR1 prices continue to rise. (Courtesy Nigel Dobbie)

Desirable options/extras

Centennial and 60th edition packs can add another x3000.
Manual gearboxes command a slightly higher price over the automatics.
LS3 cars can sell for x5000 more than the equivalent LS2.
Z51 packaged narrow-body cars can add up to x3000.
Z06 with proven head work from a reputable source, such as Lingenfelter or Katech, are sought after and add up to x5000.

The Grand Sport combines reliable LS3 with striking wide body.

Green is a non-factory color.

NPP/Bi-mode switchable exhausts, or a quality aftermarket system.
Wide-bodied Grand Sport.

Undesirable features

2005s are slightly less desirable than 2006 and later years.
Some owners prefer the reliability of the manual Convertible hood over the power hood.
Cars with Magnetic Ride Control shocks: if original, the shocks are almost certainly leaking and due a replacement.
Leather dashboards on the highest spec models are notorious for bubbling.
Highly personalised, wrapped, or heavily modified cars will narrow the market.

Value

Condition, miles, modifications, owners, transmission (manuals can be worth slightly more), specification, history and country of sale greatly influence the prices shown below. Special editions depend on all of the above, plus their numbers and desirability.

Sub x10,000. The starting point in the market are titled cars, those with significant faults or 200,000 mile narrow-body cars. There is little choice, but sometimes a bargain can be found, as in the case of the author's own clean C6.
x10,000 to x20,000 narrow-body Coupe and Convertibles, particularly 05 to 07 LS2 cars. Higher miles LS3 cars can be found in the upper teens.
x20,000 to x30,000 Good LS2 and LS3 narrow-body cars including ZHZ, with Grand Sport and Z06 very occasionally appearing closer to 30k.
x30,000 to x40,000 Low miles and late model year narrow bodies. Grand Sport and some Z06s can be found in this range.
x40,000 to x50,000 Good condition and lower miles Grand Sport and Z06.

Callaway race car is highly valuable.

x50,000 to x60,000 Lowest mileage, high specification 427, Z06 and some special editions like GT1, Ron Fellows.
x60,000 to x70,000 Titled or high miles ZR1, collector miles 427 and Z06, including carbon and Z07.
x80,000 to x110,000 ZR1 and some Callaway models, such as the C17.
x200,000+ Callaway GT4 and GT3 competition cars, Pratt and Miller C6RS.

Striking a deal

Negotiate on the basis of your assessment of condition, mileage, specification and fault rectification cost. Owners love their cars and sometimes struggle to see their C6 as an object that has no sentimental value to you, the buyer. Be realistic about the value, a small compromise on the part of the vendor or buyer will often facilitate a deal at little real cost. This is where it helps to discuss and potentially agree monies in principle, before visiting the car. Ask "What is your best price?" not, "Will you accept an offer?"

Arctic white narrow-body Coupe.

13 Do you really want to restore?

– it'll take longer and cost more than you think

You might consider a restoration if the price is very appealing, the car has a rare specification, or you just fancy a project. Just remember, though, that titled cars will always carry a stigma and lower value.

Most parts, especially those shared with other GM models are reasonably priced, whilst the cost of some C6 specific panels and electronics are occasionally an unpleasant surprise. With wide-body parts being a popular upgrade on narrow cars, the demand naturally raises prices.

Grand Sport and Z06 calipers are no longer available new from GM.

Availability of new spare parts is generally good, but with the C6 now more than two decades old, inevitably some Chevrolet items have gone out of production, or are refurbished only. This list is not exhaustive and will change: LS7 crate engines, steering racks, Z06/Grand Sport brake calipers, early year body control modules, HVAC fascia panels and some Convertible top parts are no longer available new. Aftermarket companies have and will step up where there is a demand. Used Corvette parts specialists, for example those listed in chapter 16, may be able to help.

If you're looking to restore a flood damaged car, especially involving saltwater, be aware that the fuseboard location in the passenger footwell and the engine

Aftermarket spring perch (lower) and perished original (top).

control module behind the passenger wheelarch, are both low to the ground. The floor panels are balsa wood, sandwiched between alloy (carbon fiber in the Z06/ZR1) sheets and encased in resin.

Accident damaged cars need careful assessment as to whether the SMC tubs are cracked. Steel-framed cars are easier to weld or bend if a jig is required, alloy chassis on the Z06 and ZR1 require more specialist repair.

Thankfully, rust is rarely an issue on Corvette C6s. This can partly be attributed to caring owners, with those in colder climes putting them away for the winter, and thus avoiding the ravages of road salt. Body panels don't corrode, of course, and the chassis and suspension appear well protected. Surface rust can appear on exposed fasteners, threads and bolts, but rarely enough to cause any real issue. The stainless exhausts can have mild surface rust on welds. Guide pins on Z06/Grand Sport calipers can seize, as can caliper bleed nipples on all models. Threads on lowering bolts/spring perches have been known to seize inside leaf spring ends. For those living in cold, wet climates, it's good practice to spray a penetrating oil on them periodically.

Unless you are confident with auto electrics it might be best to avoid those cars with known loom issues, for example rodent damage, or saltwater ingress, as all C6s have Canbus/Multiplex wiring (signal wire in addition to live and earth). If the car has been stored for a long time without being charged, or it has a tired battery, erroneous codes or warning lights can be thrown up.

Cars that have been previously imported to another country should have their lighting and wiring carefully checked for the quality of conversion. Remove the inner right side tail light (T15 Torx), use a mirror and flashlight and hope you don't see a rats nest of wiring and electrical tape!

If the seller tells you that the car has been partially restored, or rebuilt, then expect to be shown a series of photographs taken while the restoration was under way.

14 Paint problems

– bad complexion, including dimples, pimples and bubbles

Corvette paint is strong and durable from the factory, with all colors (even non-metallic), being covered in a protective clearcoat.

The SMC composite panels and (where relevant) carbon fiber panels are resistant to parking lot dents, springing back, often without leaving a trace. Sometimes, hours or days later, these impacts result in microcracks in the paint. They can be difficult to see, especially in the rain, and so, as a result, some owners will leave them. Check every panel carefully with a flashlight, even in bright light. Microcracks can't be polished out, the only proper cure is fresh paintwork. Harder impacts will break through, potentially leaving jagged edges. Panels can be repaired with the correct resin and fibers, followed by paint, but check for filler marks or microblisters. The exterior body panels are non-structural, so body repairs can usually be made without affecting the rigidity or safety of the car.

Microcracks are hard to see at first glance.

The low nose is vulnerable to debris thrown up from vehicles in front and from being scraped against obstacles. This is the area most likely to have received fresh paint, so check it carefully, for color match, orange peel and lacquer overspray.

Look for lines showing through

Is the bumper cover of the silver car a slightly different shade?

Ron Fellows Z06 with signature fender stripes. (Courtesy Nigel Dobbie)

the hood paintwork in the same pattern as the underhood bracing. Whilst rare, this is the result of the factory adhesive, used to bond bracing to the surface skin, causing a reaction with the original paint. Sanding back and repainting is the only cure here. The lower, trailing edges of the wheelarches are vulnerable to rock chips, but are a cosmetic concern only.

In hot climates the sun can damage clearcoat, especially those cars left outside. The clearcoat can start to peel off, especially on the hood and roof panels. When that happens, it has usually gone too far to restore with a polish. The best remedy is to strip, start again and protect using a quality wax or coating.

Paint protection film, sometimes known as a clear bra, may have been applied by a previous owner. Is it turning yellow? Older films can usually be removed without paint damage, but it takes some time to remove both the film and the adhesive.

Ceramic and graphene coatings have become a popular application, sometimes as part of a full make-over at a detailer, or they can be home applied. They won't give any protection from impact damage or stone chips, but can be a sign of a caring owner, and do give the car a glossy, long-lasting sheen.

A range of factory cars, such as the 427 heritage edition, Ron Fellows Z06, Grand Sport and Pace Car replicas, received optional vinyl stripes or decals. Some owners add styling stripes to their C6s at a later date, too. In all cases, check for fading, cracks, water marks and damage through polishing. Factory graphics can be replaced, with genuine Grand Sport stripes costing x530 and heritage stripes in excess of x1000. Reproductions are widely available for a fraction of that price. Whilst stripes can be completely removed, be aware that paint underneath may have faded over time.

When Pace car replica graphics were last sold by GM they typically cost

Pace car graphics have as many as 17 vinyl pieces. (Courtesy Nigel Dobbie)

●x2500. Phoenix Graphix in Arizona is the largest manufacturer of licensed restoration graphics kits, and should be able to help with 2007 and 2008 Indy Pace Car reproduction vinyl, at a cost of ●x600. A quality shop specializing in vehicle graphics may be able to reproduce individual vinyl graphics from high resolution photos.

A vinyl wrap can give a car a completely new look, but can leave a buyer with an element of doubt about what might be lurking underneath. Ask the seller for photos of the car before/during the wrapping process. A quality wrap can give a unique look that lasts for many years and actually protects the paint underneath. A poorly applied, or old wrap, especially one applied on top of existing damage, can look fine from 20 feet, but reveal bubbles, peeling, poor adhesion and errors on close inspection.

Aftermarket stripes – check the vinyl for marks.

15 Problems due to lack of use

– just like their owners, Corvettes need exercise!

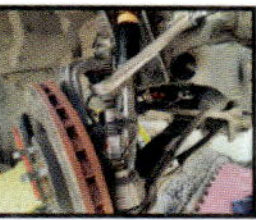

Cars, like humans, are at their most efficient if they exercise regularly. This isn't always possible, however, for cars kept in areas with long, harsh winters, and others that are brought out only for occasional runs, in the nicest weather.

Electrics

A failing battery (and some, non-oem alternators) can throw up all sorts of spurious warnings and codes, unrelated to the root cause of the battery! Bad earths can also cause a little head scratching until sourced, but, usually, a cleanup of the chassis points is all that's needed. Corvette C6s will drain a battery within a few weeks if not started; using a quality battery tender or trickle charger is essential if the car is stored with the battery connected. Leave the hood open slightly, so the battery or electrical jump post can be accessed without having to resort to the emergency trunk key.

2005 manual transmission cars must be placed in reverse when parked, to avoid battery drain.

Tire pressure monitors (TPMS)

These are located within each valve and contain a small battery. They can last ten years, but once the battery runs low they will show XX on the DIC, preventing the selection of competitive driving mode. Having the tire removed from the rim, sensor replaced and reprogrammed to the car is the answer. TPMS are from x30 each, and the simple tool to reprogramme them from x10. 2005 to 2009 and 2010 to 2013 require different sensors and tool, with European models operating on a different frequency from the US cars.

Tire manufactured in late 2023.

Tires

Tires that have had the weight of the car on them in a single position for some time will develop flat spots, resulting in some (usually temporary) vibration. The tire walls may have cracks or (blister-type) bulges, or just be too old. Anything older than 5 or 6 years will have a gradual drop in grip and performance, even if they have covered few miles. If the car is exposed to a lot of sunlight (UV), a tire may need to be replaced sooner, certainly well before dry-rot sets in.

Rubber and plastic

Window, door and roof seals can harden and leak. Gaitors/boots can crack on the CV joints and ends of the steering rack. Wiper blades will harden. The lowering bolt spring perch threads can seize with rust and the rubber and steel layers that contact the lower wishbones can perish and separate.

Fluids

Old brake fluid with a high water content can cause corrosion at the bleed nipple(s) and, more seriously, can cause significant brake fade in high-stress braking scenarios. Ideally change this every two years, regardless of miles.

Fuel will go bad in a matter of months. A stabilizer added to the plastic fuel tanks can help, but the best solution is to flush the fuel system before starting and replace with quality, high octane gas. There is no external fuel filter, it is fitted inside the tank.

Highly modified cars converted to run on E85 flex fuel, then left unused for long periods, will have problems with the fuel solidifying.

Oil will drain down from the heads and cylinder walls, creating friction on that first start. If the oil and filter are old, change them, same for the sparkplugs. Whilst the plugs are out, a drop of two stroke oil (that burns cleanly) in each sparkplug hole will help provide temporary cylinder wall lubrication. Place your foot firmly on the throttle pedal and attempt to start in the usual way. Provided the gas pedal is fully depressed, the engine won't fire, but it will turn over, building oil pressure as it cranks.

Miscellaneous

Rodents can be a nightmare in any stored car; their little teeth create havoc with rubber hoses and underhood electrics, not to mention the mess and smell if they get inside the cabin! Look for tell-tale gnaw marks and droppings.

Seized components are rare but possible, including pistons in callipers, clutch or flexplate to flywheel, and handbrakes (parking brakes) if the cables rust.

With lack of use, the shock absorbers/dampers will lose their elasticity or even seize. Creaking, groaning and stiff suspension are suggestive of this problem. Magnetic Ride Control shocks particularly are known to leak.

Replace old, leaking dampers with quality units, like KW.

16 The Community

– key people, organisations and companies in the C6 world

Clubs

The Corvette community is a big part of ownership, be it collective knowledge shared online, local meets, or club events. There are literally hundreds of Corvette clubs around the world, with the largest concentration being in the United States.

Z06 Carbon Edition outside the NCM. (Courtesy Nigel Dobbie)

Your C6 is displayed on the Corvette Boulevard, as part of the NCM Experience.

The National Corvette Museum (NCM), Bowling Green, Kentucky, is one place that every Corvette owner and enthusiast should visit. This famous museum, complete with sinkhole story, store and diner, has enough to keep you busy for a day, especially if the factory tour and nearby NCM Motorsports Park are accessible. The museum hosts a number of huge events, including the BASH and Corvette Caravan. Check the online calendar for dates of the largest tours and meets around the nation.

The 'NCM experience' is available for Corvettes of all ages. Costing around

Add some numbers and go and have some fun on the track, your C6 was made for it.

Cold air intake, just be careful of flood water.

●x500, it includes checks, valet, photo, factory tour and your car parked in the museum avenue, a special experience. C6s handed over new from the NCM had the 'R8C' factory collection code on the build sheet.

Corvettes at Carlisle, Pennsylvania, is the largest international Corvette meet, with up to 3000 cars of all years attending each year.

Track days/high performance driving experiences

Every C6, regardless of the model, is capable of being driven on track – I urge you to consider it; the C6 is a capable platform straight out of the box. These track days/HPDE are non-competitive, educational events that take place on race circuits all over the world, where you learn the limits of your own car, without speed limits, pedestrians or oncoming traffic!

Social media and the web

C6 social media groups and forums are a great place to share photos, experiences

Fast 102 intake helps all LS engines breathe, but particularly the LS2.

and parts for sale. Search engines will link to various DIY guides and how-tos, with YouTube being a valuable resource. It should be added that there are plenty of oft-repeated myths and unresearched opinions within some of the review videos, something I discovered whilst researching this book.

Lightweight alloy flywheel helps the revs rise and fall much quicker.

Tuning and modifying

The C6 has proved to be an incredible platform to tune and modify. There is an abundance of companies and parts that can improve or change your car. Large US-based companies selling stock and upgraded parts internationally include Zip, Rock Auto, Summit, Mid America Motorworks and JEGS.

Common upgrades include muffler changes for more noise and long-tube headers for a noticeable bump of power and noise. Combined with a cold air intake and custom tune, this can net around 40hp. The tune improves automatic shifts, torque management, fan temperatures, intake air temperature table and more. A FAST 102 intake manifold adds another 20HP to LS2 engines, replacing the restrictive stock item.

All LS have a single camshaft and respond well to a cam change, together

Supercharging delivers a big bang for your buck.

with supporting modifications like stronger valve springs, rocker bearings and hardened pushrods. The cam, combined with intake, exhaust and tune changes listed above, typically gains 50 to 100hp over stock or more. Cams from Brian Tooley Racing, Lingenfelter, LG Motorsports, Katech, COMP Cams and more are all available with different characteristics to suit your car.

An aggressive cam will require automatics to be fitted with a performance torque convertor, with higher stall speed.

Stock clutches are robust to about 550-600hp, the LS7 and LS9 clutch are stronger again and are a popular upgrade to LS2 and LS3 engines, but requiring a little more left leg effort. Once power exceeds 600hp, or sticky tires exploited, then Monster or Mantic twin or triple clutches are recommended. Changing the differential final drive in both auto and manual cars can certainly liven up the acceleration feel, shortening the long ratios that are fitted to all but the Z51 equipped cars. Getting the correct ring and pinion meshing requires professional set up, tools and parts.

LS engines respond well to forced induction, with single and twin turbo chargers, or bolt on superchargers from Vortech, Magnusson, A&A and ECS a cost-effective way of adding serious horsepower to your C6. At least a 150HP to 200HP gain is normal, on a stock LS2 or LS3 engine, with a supercharger and custom tune only. Complete kits start from x5500. You may find that you'll want to upgrade a few other parts to compliment this, including cooling, brakes, tires and clutch, but the stock engine components seem to comfortably take this sort of power increase with few issues. Considerably more power (1000hp+) is available if your wallet and heart can take it!

Brake pads and fresh fluid can improve stopping performance and feel, with Mintex, EBC, Powerstop, Carbotech and Hawk well regarded. Big brake kits from AP Racing (Essex), Brembo, Wilwood and Alcon all deliver repeated stopping power. Owners of narrow-body cars can retrofit the Grand Sport/Z06 brakes, or (with a little work) the Cadillac ATS/Brembo front calipers. Most bigger brakes will either require spacers or different wheels on the narrow-body cars.

Suspension can be lowered; all C6s from the factory had composite, monoleaf springs front and rear, with adjustable spring perches. To raise or lower each corner, you need a floor jack or two, stands and a 10mm wrench. Dampers from KW, Bilstein, Koni or Doug Rippie each have different firmness, adjustability and price Alternatively, for those wanting to replace the monoleafs, you can jump to coilovers. If your car has Magnetic Ride Control and wish to move to a conventional damper, you will either need plug in simulators, or have their function deleted using a Tech 2, otherwise you will have a DIC speed limit warning.

Wide-body panels can be fitted to a narrow-body car for looks and to

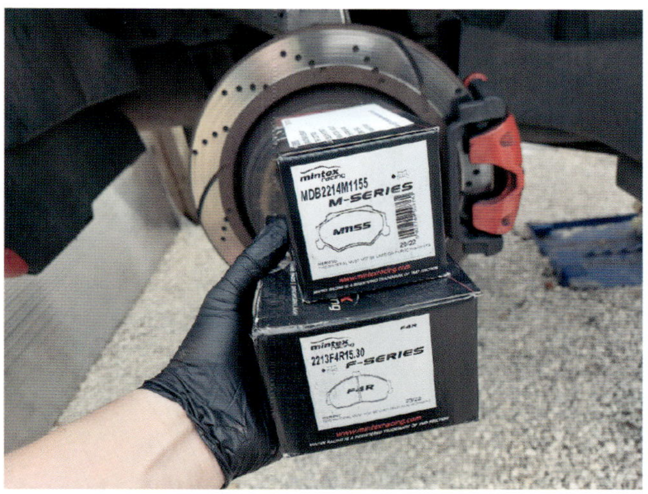

Quality pads to help your Corvette stop.

Corbeau Evolution X are designed to fit specifically into the C5 and C6 cabin.

accommodate wider wheels and tires. C7 Stingray wheels and rear C5 Z06 wheels are an alternative design that fits narrow bodied cars, for those wanting to stick with GM. Quality wheels, from Apex, CCW or Forgeline are often lighter, higher strength and available in widths and offsets for both the narrow and wide-bodied C6.

Seats with enhanced lateral support are available from Corbeau and Caravaggio, or go further, with full race seats, combined with low mounts from AMT. The C6 tunnel shape makes fitting wider sports seats a challenge. C7 and C8 seats can be retrofitted, with electric functionality too.

Turn One Steering (https://turnonesteering.com) provides a steering rebuild service.

Knightdrivetv.com makes a large 'Max-din' touch screen, that replaces both the climate and stereo units.

Crane's Corvette Supply, San Diego, CA 92111, stocks a bewildering array of upgrades, components and accessories, and even cars (www.cranescorvettesupply.com).

Sharp Light Innovations stocks a wide range of lighting upgrades (Sharplightinnovations.com).

Manuals, how tos

Comprehensive, printed GM workshop manuals are available in multiple volumes, from NCM store, Zip Corvette and other sources.

Haynes, and Chilton manuals, that cover both C5 and C6 models, are not as comprehensive as the factory manuals.

More reading

• *The Corvette Black Book* is highly recommended as the go-to resource to establish facts and figures. The 70th anniversary 1953-2023 2nd edition is the last planned publication in the range. ISBN 978-0933534667
• *Corvette The Rise Of A Sports Car*, by Mark Eaton is a well-written background for all Corvettes, including how the C5 evolved into the C6. ISBN 978-1445664453
• *Corvette C6*, by Phil Berg, was published in 2004, on the eve of the launch of the C6. It doesn't have any details of later C6 derivatives, editions or engines, but delivers quality photos and diagrams. ISBN 978-0760318652
• Each model year had a glossy dealer brochure, many of which can still be purchased new, from the NCM store, as well as other online sources.
• For the younger C6 enthusiasts, this author has written a range of 'Clive The Corvette' illustrated children's books, based on the real adventures he and his C6 have enjoyed in the USA, Europe and Africa. Available to buy in the NCM store.

17 Vital statistics
– essential data at your fingertips

Narrow/standard-width body
2005 Coupe and Convertible, 5967cc/364ci LS2, 4 AT or MN6.
400hp, 400lb/ft
2006-2007 Coupe and Convertible, 5967cc/364ci LS2, 6 AT or MN6.
400hp, 400lb/ft
2008-2013 Coupe and Convertible, 6162cc/376ci LS3, 6 AT or MN6.
430hp, 424lb/ft

Wide-body
2006-2013 Z06 fixed roof Coupe, 7011cc/427cu LS7, MN6.
505hp, 470lb/ft
2009-2013 ZR1 fixed roof Coupe, 6162cc/376ci LS9, MN6.
638hp, 604lb/ft
2010-2013 Grand Sport Coupe and Convertible, 6162cc/376ci LS3, 6 AT or MN6.
430hp, 424lb/ft
2013 427 Convertible, 7011cc/427cu LS7, MN6.
505hp, 470lb/ft

Final year, 427 Convertible, with 60th anniversary stripes. (Courtesy James Langille)

Statistics (note that options and model years vary in weight)
Model/0-60mph in seconds/Maximum Speed in mph/Length in inches/Width in inches/Height in inches/Curb weight in pounds

Narrow-/standard-width body
2005-2007 LS2/ 4.1 (Z51 MN6), 4.2 (MN6), 4.5 (4AT)/186/174.6/72.6/49.1/3179

(Coupe), 3199 (Convertible)
2008-2013 LS3/ 4.1 (MN6), 4.3 6AT)/190/other stats similar to above

Wide-body

2010+ Grand Sport LS3/ 4.0 (MN6 Coupe), 4.4 (6AT Convertible)/175.6/75.9/49/3311 (Coupe), 3289 (Convertible).
2006+ Z06 LS7/ 3.7 (MN6)/199/175.6/75.9/49/3132
2009+ ZR1 LS9/ 3.4 (MN6)/205/175.6/75.9/49/3324

Fuel tank - 18 US Gallons   Turning Circle - 39ft

2007 was the largest production year, with 40,561 cars produced. Red, in various shades was the best-selling color. Narrow body models, Coupe in particular, are the most numerous, with automatic transmissions fitted to more than half of these.

Total C6 Production: 215,123

Lowered Z06 on large wheels.

Having this book in your pocket is just like having a real marque expert by your side. Benefit from the author's years of Corvette C2 ownership (he's bought and sold more than 700!), learn how to spot a bad car quickly and how to assess a promising one like a professional. Get the right car at the right price!

ISBN: 978-1-845843-29-8
Paperback • 19.5x13.9cm • 64 pages • 105 pictures

For more information and price details, visit our website at www.veloce.co.uk • email: info@veloce.co.uk

The Essential Buyer's Guide
S-CLASS

The Essential Buyer's Guide
Mercedes-Benz
SL

The Essential Buyer's Guide
Mercedes-Benz
SLK

The Essential Buyer's Guide
Mercedes-Benz
W123

The Essential Buyer's Guide
Mercedes-Benz
W124

The Essential Buyer's Guide
MG & Austin-Healey
MIDGET & SPRITE

The Essential Buyer's Guide
MG
TD, TF & TF1500

The Essential Buyer's Guide
MG
MGA

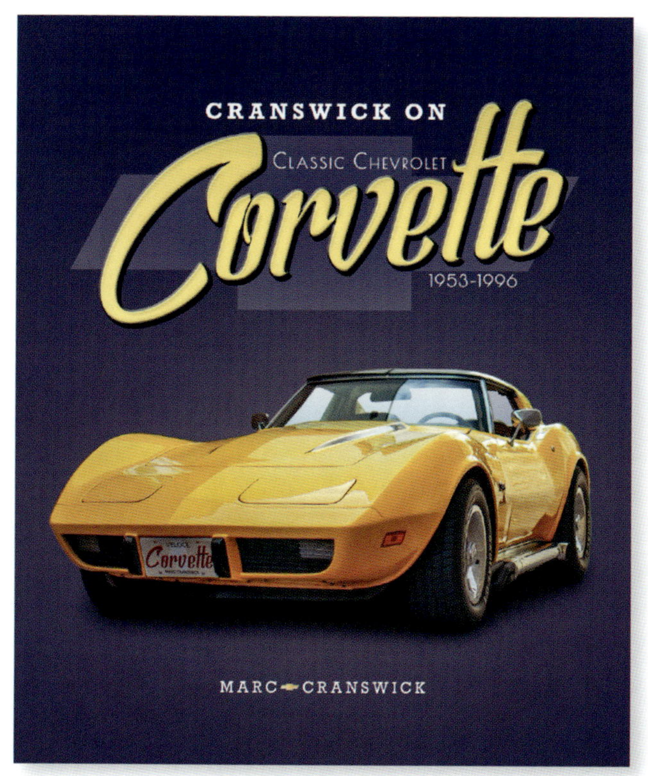

This book charts the rise of America's only sports car: the Chevrolet Corvette. Its performance, sales and racing achievements are chronicled against a backdrop of industry commentators and key GM and Chevrolet figures; a pictorial presentation of the Plastic Fantastic, depicting its global high performance impact.

ISBN: 978-1-787119-08-6
Hardback • 25x20.7cm • 240 pages • 425 colour and b&w pictures

For more information and price details, visit our website at www.veloce.co.uk • email: info@veloce.co.uk

Index

Z06 at Laguna Seca.

Organized club road trips enhance ownership experiences.
(Courtesy Chris Blewett)

KANSAS
US
66

Notes